The

BURDEN

of a

MAN

*A Biblical perspective to generational cycles of rebellion
that have been normalized*

ELIYAH I. BRITTO

i

Publishing in the United States of America
Publisher: Luminous Publishing
www.luminouspublishing.com
For bulk orders or other inquiries, email:
info@luminouspublishing.com

Contents

Dedication

This book is dedicated to all the women and little girls who are suffering in silence, fighting to not become a product of their environment. To all those who will choose to be The One no matter how far gone you think you are. My beloved sister and friend, now is the time to confront negative cycles and put them to rest...forever. This is the time to dismantle cycles that are hindering you from your destiny and to be set apart. I pray this book aids you in walking in your God given identity and authority; becoming a healthier you physically, mentally, emotionally and spiritually.

Acknowledgements

I want to thank my amazing husband Joseph, for his continued love, support, hard work and dedication. Your character is unmatched and I am so grateful God allowed us to become one. You have not only been a great contributor to this book but, you have also been a great contributor to the woman I am and am becoming. Your selflessness is convicting and your humility is inspiring. I'm privileged to get back stage access to the life you are building for us, our future children and generations to come. I love you so much babe!

I want to thank my lovely mother Tracy, who is the epitome of resilience and grace. Without your patience and tough love, I'm not sure where I would be today. I saw the sacrifices, the silent tears and the silent prayers for a child who you just needed to act right! Well "How does she pause now? [insider]." I love you mom and I can't wait for you to grace this world with all you have to offer!

Last but certainly not least, I want to thank my awesome Publisher, Karolyne Roberts and the entire Luminous Publishing team. You guys have been so helpful and so amazing. You are truly a God send and I would not have it any other way!

1

Introduction

I would love to begin by asking a question I have always pondered on: How many of us grew up with a single mother? For me, it's a life that I know all too well. Being raised by a single mother and single women in general, had a negative impact on my view of submission and independence. A cycle of resistance and rebellion towards men began to take root in my heart without me realizing it. I thought it made me a *woman* and that it was the *norm* to take over and tell the man what to do. I would always have this thought *He won't do it right or he doesn't know what he's doing,* which became my way of reasoning. I thought it was normal to do whatever I wanted with no regard for the feelings of a man. Over time, I grew to think that I was supposed to make it very clear to any man that I am the only boss of me.

Rebellion toward men leading was very prevalent in my environment and submission was something I wasn't accustomed to. The only example of submission I had was the scene in the movie, *Coming to America,* when the woman who was arranged to marry Prince Hakeem did EVERYTHING he told her to do, no matter how silly it was. I know that sounds funny but that was my idea of submission. Many people, especially women, cringe at the very word "submission." We view it like the scene in *Coming to America*; as giving up our identity and dignity for a *man*.

However, the true meaning and practice of submission is far from the negative connotations of the word itself. The ability to submit or not comes down to one's understanding of submission, heart posture, and alignment with God's Word. But don't worry, we will get into that later on in the book. Just know that once the true meaning of submission is understood and the action of headship is demonstrated correctly, we will begin to see and know its power and importance on a higher level.

Growing up, I saw a lot of dysfunctional relationships. Consequently, it wasn't too long before I ended up in some of my own. Any slight appearance of a guy trying to show authority or *lead* me in any way always resulted in an argument and an "I can do bad all by myself" attitude. I felt that a man's effort to help me was a disguise to control or handicap me. To me, showing any need for his help was an act of desperation and a sign of weakness. I was taught that you should never let a man do things for you because he will use that against you to get what he wants from you. I was told to always have a stash of money he doesn't know about just in case something doesn't work out. I was taught that my needs and feelings were priorities that needed to be met and that since he was *the man*, he should be able to take whatever I threw at him. If he didn't, then he was weak and I needed to move on. Back then, I didn't realize how that screamed nothing but inconsideration, toxicity, dysfunction, and selfishness.

But all the above is the complete opposite of God's design for headship and submission. I'm sure you may have heard these things too, whether from personal experience or from someone else's story. Whichever way you may have also encountered that type of mindset or advice, I'm here to debunk and transform those thoughts in an attempt to challenge how you view the role of a man in relationships. I'm here to encourage you to examine any self-destructive behaviors that may have stemmed from your childhood, which now impacts the way you view and interact with the opposite sex.

There's no doubt that, from a historical perspective, women have often been mistreated by men. As a result, submission to a male figure has become a complicated and challenging practice. However, when spiritual leadership is exercised correctly, submission should come easily.

This book is coming from a transparent and sincere place of demonstrating that transformation in my life. I understand that some of these perspectives and statements may rub people the wrong way and I am also aware that there are issues that need to be addressed directly with the men — I get it! However, in my journey, I have come to learn the importance of self-reflection and evaluation. I cannot tell someone how they have damaged or hurt me before I address how I allowed that very hurt and pain to bleed on to others and ruin relationships.

> "Hypocrite! First remove the plank from your own
> eye, and then you will see clearly to remove the speck
> from your brother's eye" (Matthew 7:5 NKJV).

It may not be the most popular view, especially in today's radically feminist society, but if we want to truly get out of toxic relational cycles, we need to be aware of and understand the biblical structure of marriage and how our families or upbringing play a major role in our character today.

2

The Rebellious Woman

Six months before our wedding, my fiancé quit his job. Fear, worry, and doubt had every right to run rampant in my life and I could have easily let it. However, that was a season where I was being intentional about really trusting God beyond what I could see. So, I took this as a test, prayed for peace, and supported his decision. To be honest, I wasn't opposed to him leaving his job. The salary was very helpful, to say the least, bearing in mind that we had our respective bills that would soon become one, a wedding coming around the corner, and a goal to purchase a home shortly after our wedding. However, the toll his job had on him was not worth it. I didn't want to go into a marriage with a burned-out spouse and he didn't want to be a semi-present husband.

We were on the same page and decided to trust God on another level. If all I cared about was having my needs met and our special *day*, I could've turned into the quarrelsome wife-to-be that Proverbs 25:24 speaks about. I could have guilted him into staying at his job, or, made him feel less than *a man* because he walked out of a prestigious corporate position. But what would that have done? He already resented his job and that resentment possibly could have been redirected towards me because he would only continue to work there to make me *feel* happy and secure. Negative! I've learned that my security is not in a paycheck or in a man's ability. I also could not stand seeing him drained from work, getting text and emails day-in, day-out, during vacations, holidays, and weekends. Plus, that took away a lot of time from me — and I wasn't having that. Lol.

In all seriousness, I've learned that choosing to be supportive over condemning goes a long way, especially when it comes to spouses. On top of that, I was able to identify that time in our relationship as a season where my words, response, and actions really mattered. What I said and how I said things could either break him down or build him up. As Kingdom children, we should always be in the building-up business and the only tearing down we should be doing are strongholds. Did fear or doubt ever kick in? Yea! A man you're about to marry not working full-time? Come on, we already know how that is perceived, especially for a *black* man. (If that offends you, that is not the intent. I am just speaking **our** truth.) But there are already so many factors and private battles he has to fight being a black man alone, so why would I make our relationship another battlefield? Having to fight the world is one thing, but having to sharpen your sword to prepare for war at home is another. Things like this can cause silent depression and coldness from our spouse or significant other. They already live in constant war with their surroundings and even with their own thoughts or insecurities. However, when the one place that is supposed to serve as their safety zone has hidden mines of its own, your home will be the very last place he runs to for cover.

Knowing how pivotal my words and demonstration of support in this season would be, I decided to go above and beyond, showing my trust and support of him. I had peace knowing that he wasn't just leaving to be leaving. It was for his betterment and overall health AND…he had a plan. That was key. If he didn't have a plan, we would have had an entirely different conversation.

I'm not encouraging you to put up with a man who is always making big decisions with no fruit from the last. I'm not encouraging you to put up with empty dreams that he has not made any PLANS or ACTIONS for. However, I am only encouraging you to ask questions if you're worried. BUT, there is a way to ask questions. Some of us haven't quite mastered the art of asking but have mastered the art of concluding very well. You know how well we can do that. We already have the answer in our head, so we begin to form our questions in a way that will confirm that answer, thereby making us *right*. Especially if he didn't run his decision by you and you want to be able to say, "I told you so!"

When our men make big decisions that we feel should have been run by us first or they don't take heed to our input, we tend to create an atmosphere of discomfort with our words alone. For example, we say things like "So, when you left your job, did you leave your common sense there too?" Or "These bills didn't get started independently, so I don't expect them to be paid independently." Then, to add insult to injury, we throw in sly remarks which make him feel small and inadequate, such as, "So, since we're quitting jobs now, can you quit leaving your dirty laundry laying around the house?" Or if he reaches for the last of something in the fridge, we say, "Are you going to buy more?" You may have some examples of your own but I hope you get the point I want to make here. Plainly put, we just become Petty Betty.

On the surface, we may not see the impact of our words because he just shrugs it off, ignores you, or walks away. But I can guarantee you that the seeds of those words will sprout weeds in different areas of your marriage, such as sex, communication, intimacy, and even the way he sees or looks at you. These types of questions, remarks, and the likes are NOT conducive to the feelings of inadequacy, fear, or anxiety he may already be dealing with. If he seems to not have a plan, help him. I want to stress the word HELP because our idea of *help* can come off as TELLING him what to do, which often doesn't leave room for what he wants to do. I like to call it *help-telling*. We have to learn how to put an end to help-telling our spouses. When you help someone, both voices matter. He just may have a plan but is hesitant to reveal it to you because you constantly shoot down his ideas and make him feel like what he says is dumb or pointless. Have you ever felt like you were so close to someone and that that person would tell you their biggest dreams? You give them advice about everything and you always tell them what you think they should do when they are in a dilemma. You didn't even notice that they never asked for your input but you inserted yourself anyway and it threw them off. Imagine if this same person told a mutual friend they received this big offer on a product they have been developing and the only way you found out was secondhand by that mutual friend.

So, you ask, "Why didn't you tell me?

And they respond by saying, "Well, I tried but every time I told you about something, you gave me your opinion instead of asking me how I felt about it."

Now, you find yourself having to eat your words. Really think about that. If he feels he has no support from you because you jump to your opinion before hearing his heart about a thing, why then would he seek to confide his dreams in you?

We, as women, especially now more than ever, are go-getters and we dare anyone to try to tell us what we can and can't do, and we will buck at anyone who tries to. So, how do you think your spouse feels when you try to tell him what he can, can't, or should do? Do you think he wants you to tear down his dreams, ideas, or desires? Do you think telling him he can't or what's not possible is a way of *saving* him from failure? Treat him how you would want to be treated. Better yet, support him how you would want or expect him to support you. No matter how dumb you think it may be, that's HIS dream, NOT yours. You have no right to shoot it down. If he's not doing anything that is sinful or displeases God, go help him to achieve that… *help*meet.

This may sound funny but, if that man wanted to burn CDs and sell them out the back of his trunk like they did back in the day, then you better be out there with him promoting those CDs, or at least putting the covers on them. You're probably saying, "Eliyah, this is so unrealistic! It's 2020! No one burns CDs anymore and that's just wack!" Well, guess what? A lot of ideas may seem wack until you apply some creativity and pressure to it. Instead of shooting it down, flip that idea and make it 2020 RELEVANT. Period. Get creative. This would be a creative flip: "Hey babe, since a lot of people are streaming music now, what do you think about opening a vintage music spot and we can have throwback events on Saturdays? That way, people can get that old school feel and be more inclined to buy music the old school way."

Boom! Do you see where I'm going? Adjust the dreams and ideas as time goes on because everything evolves and comes right back around in a relevant form. The dreams CAN work;

you just have to work them. Don't shoot his idea down straight off the bat. Listen to what his ideas or goals are, ask questions, and ask him how you can help him fulfill his goals. That is music to a man's ears! "What! She supports me, she believes I can do this? Bet, now I really gotta go get this."

Side note: Now, don't get me wrong. Supporting him does not mean your life, dreams, and desires have come to an end. You both can achieve your goals and help one another get to the top. If he doesn't want to see you win as well, he definitely has some testosterone issues that go beyond you. But I have to save that for another book!

When he sees how supportive you are, that will allow him to feel safe and confident in revealing his unspoken dreams and aspirations to you — the ones he normally keeps hidden for fear of being over-scrutinized. He will begin to trust that you are in his corner versus depending on you to be the voice of rejection. Not only that, you just simultaneously boosted his confidence in a major way, which will prompt him to apply even more pressure because he doesn't want to disappoint you. Do you see that? Our support makes our men go harder for the win, in turn, making us win too! You never know, his idea can be *the next big thing,* but you just killed it with your doubts and judgments before he was able to birth or walk it out.

I know it's not easy having an unstable home, wondering how bills are going to be paid. I know what it's like when the last thing you thought was secure is no longer solid. To be transparent, there was a time where my now husband's, "We can't afford that right now" went from me being *understanding* to me being frustrated. It triggered a full range of negative emotions due to the lack I had in my childhood. When the job situation first happened, I was excited to be on board. He continued to do his notary business on the side and picked up more hours at a gym he worked at on and off. I started saving more aggressively and got creative with our date nights, knowing that they would look a little different than usual.

Then all of a sudden, his "Not right now...," "After the wedding...," and "I can't..." just got louder and louder and I hit my breaking point... right in the parking lot of Shoppers. Yes, Shoppers! I drove to the grocery store after work, but before I got out of the car, I realized I didn't have my wallet. So, I called Joseph to see if I had left it with him. He said no and then I remembered that I left it at work and was not about to drive back to get it. Now, in these types of situations, I was used to him saying, "Don't worry about it babe; where are you? I'll come meet you to give you my card or just transfer you the money" without me having to ask. But this time, that didn't happen and I got upset. I didn't express my feelings to him at the moment but I was burning with built-up frustration on the inside. I began to mentally add up all his no's and not right now's and became angry at myself for getting *comfortable* with him *saving* me. I started to go back into my Rebellious Woman mindset and thought of all the reasons to never depend on him again or any man. That may seem extreme to some and understandable to a few, but this was my reality.

That moment was the moment I feared would happen when I *chose* to let him lead; me not being able to depend on him, and him disappointing me. It was a mentality that I fought so hard to let go of and when I finally let go of it, it was tested and I wanted to kick myself. All the "I told you so's" from the women I grew up with started to scream in my head. For a moment, I felt like I had let them down for depending on the man who would soon be my husband. Doesn't that sound crazy? I was supposed to feel like I could depend on him, ESPECIALLY since he was about to be my husband.

The dysfunctions of our past have a strange way of arousing guilt in us, making us believe that we will never live beyond our past because of *one* disappointment. Nope! I had to shake myself and talk back to those voices with the Word of God. I had to remind myself that his situation was only temporary, and most importantly, that no marriage is absent of disappointments. I had to be prepared to extend grace beyond what I felt. This is the man that I wanted to be with for the rest of my life; for richer or for poorer. Also, since that is the decision I was making, I could not go back to the old Eliyah's mindset. I could not go back into previous relationship habits of trying to wear the pants and making him feel less of a man just because he couldn't bring me his credit card that day.

When I accepted that engagement ring, I accepted God's order of marriage. A man is the head of the woman and that equation had no room for my old way of thinking. I had to remind myself that this was the man I loved and would do anything for and that he would do the SAME for me too. I also had to ask myself, how would it make him feel if I expressed my frustration at his temporary inability to help right now, especially in that moment. I knew him well enough to safely assume that he probably already felt like crap because he couldn't be the superman he was used to and enjoyed being to me. Why would I add to that feeling? Not that I would never bring it up at a later time for open conversation but, at that moment, it just was not a wise decision.

Remember, our responses are vital. I could've opened a whole can of worms that led to hurtful words becoming a forever bruise on his heart and mine, even after the "I'm sorry." I gave up bruising egos a long time ago. It's not worth it. It doesn't feel good and it should never feel good to break down someone you *love*. How many forever bruises have you left on your spouse's heart because of emotions you just *had* to let out about his lack of _____ (you fill in the blank) in a moment where silence was *your* weapon and *his* cure?

You couldn't talk yourself into stepping away, getting your emotions together and then seeing if it was worth addressing? Nine times out of ten, when we step away before breathing fire and calm down to **THINK** about how and why we feel the way we do, we often realize that it wasn't worth the anger. It could have been addressed in a non-confrontational manner that would avoid arguments and chaos.

Now, you may be saying that everything is an argument. No matter how you say what you need or want to say, your spouse always construes it as "You just want to argue." I get that. Men can sometimes interpret our comments as a desire to argue when that is NOT the case. Joseph and I have had our share of battles with that too. But for us, I realized that was his defense mechanism to beat me to the punch. He was used to me starting off calm when I expressed my feelings and then blowing up the moment he said something I didn't agree with, or if I felt his response was a result of him not understanding or listening to me.

So, what I learned to do was retrain the way he hears my conversations. Before the retraining, I had to retrain myself and identify the flaws in the way I communicated. Through this, I was able to admit, "Hey babe, I know in the past I would say this and react that way but, I know that never ends well and I want us to grow in that area. I understand that you expect me to react in a certain way when I don't feel you hear me but, moving forward, I want us to have stronger communication. What would help you hear me better?"

Yes, I know, it seems like you have to be a doormat or shrink yourself, right? Well, if you feel that way, you are most definitely entitled to your opinion, just as I am. This is one of the reasons why I wrote this book. If we continue to have that perspective instead of seeing the strength that is demonstrated when we humble ourselves, we will never see the beauty of Kingdom marriages. We will never see the beauty of why God created and designed us the way that He did because we're so blinded by pride and don't want to be the one that has to *give* in order to *get*. How we come to our spouse should resemble the way we come to God, which should be with humility and honor. If you continue to walk in prideful loftiness and approach your spouse any kind of way, you'll continue to be enraged at him because he may not be *listening* or changing. He will continue to seek fulfillment and appreciation elsewhere, while only simply tolerating you and possibly never coming home while you're awake. I know that is a little tough, but it's the reality for some of us.

Someone has got to give. Why not just start with you? You are the only person who you have control of to change, anyway. You only waste your strength, time, and energy trying to change anyone else. Work on yourself, give your husband to the Lord and watch how the Lord works. If you are experiencing communication turmoil or any difficulties in your marriage, I'm declaring that you will see a change in your marriage bigger than you've ever desired or expected in Jesus' name. Once you let go, don't pick it back up. Trust God and let Him do what He needs to do in **both** your life and that of your husband.

3

Any Time, Any Place

In high school, I remember walking from Chick-Fil-A with a guy I was dating at the time. He was a member of the football team while I was on the Poms team. It was fun because technically, none of the players were allowed to be out on a game day, especially not with a girl. But we were sure enough out and about. Anyway, we were trying to make it back to school before our coaches noticed, but we ended up arguing along the way because I saw something on his phone that I didn't like. He tried to assure me that it was *nothing* and made me feel like I was overreacting. So, I then assured him that if he didn't stop acting like I was blind, I was going to knock his head off.

To paint a better picture, the walk from CFA back to school wasn't far but it was next to a transit station and other stores. It was a very open and public place to walk and the last place you would want to be seen on your worst behavior because someone who either knew your mother, sister or brother would be somewhere watching. But that didn't stop me from letting him have it. Everyone driving past saw my rage and it wasn't too long before a phone ended up being thrown down the sidewalk and into the street. I say "a phone" because I honestly don't remember if it was mine or his—crazy I know! Why would I break my own stuff, right? Don't judge me!

Fast forward to the next day, I saw him talking in the hallway with the same girl, who he was texting the day before and was sharing his banana pudding with her from the same spoon! In my head, I began to think, "This boy has really lost his mind." Even though he didn't notice me watching, one of his friends did and tapped him on the shoulder to look my way. He was *shook* to say the least. But, I didn't react right there and then, which I think made him more nervous. I did an *okay bet* head nod and walked my butt to class. After school, he met me at my locker trying to explain himself. I just made him take my bag and let him talk. Even though I was upset, I wanted to hear how he would try to make me *think* I'm crazy this time when I know he saw me clearly looking at them. Then he said the silliest thing I have ever heard, "She just ate off my spoon; it's not like I kissed her or nothing" — and there went my mind. I lost it, again.

Needless to say, we had very public arguments and that same behavior pattern of short tempers and poor self-control growing up followed me into different aspects and relationships throughout my life. Looking back on it all, it is not a way I would ever want to be remembered. Even though my frustrations were warranted, my reactions could have been a lot different and *less* public. The whole world did not need to know what was going on in my relationship(s) and I owed it to myself to have more dignity and class. Even though I can't change those situations, I thank God for growing me in those areas.

Over the years, in my journey of self-reflection, I realized that I did not always take the right approach when addressing a situation. I wouldn't think until AFTER and by that time, feelings were hurt, emotions were numb, and pride was at a high, so apologies were rarely spoken. I would go in with the mindset of, "I'm about to hit him where it hurts" versus, "I'm going to remain calm." I never thought I had to. I thought being angry granted me the right to show it how I wanted to. I never saw the *calm* way to handle hurt growing up. So, I did what I knew to do.

When I got hurt in relationships, their feelings didn't matter anymore. They automatically became my enemy. I made up in my mind that they were going to feel the pain ten times harder so they'd know not to hurt me again. I wasn't going to relent until I felt *better*. What I've come to learn is that if you have to hurt someone else just to make yourself feel better, you have created your own danger zone, and no one can be safe around you. Some of you may not even realize that you hit low just to make yourself feel better. You're so used to doing it that it has become a part of your *reaction*.

You may be thinking, no, just don't hurt me and we're good. Well, there's an issue with that because your definition of hurt may not meet someone else's. If they do something that *hurts* you unbeknownst to them, they'll have to pay for your inability to cope and communicate pain in a healthy way. If you can truly only feel better by fighting fire with fire, then you will continue to be a walking flame. There are always going to be times and people that do or say things that might offend you, and if you can't change how you allow it to affect you, you will never be a better you. You can't control others, so reacting with fire will just make matters worse and make you look just as foolish as they may be. Proverbs 26:4 says, *"Don't answer the foolish arguments of fools, or you will become as foolish as they are."*

How do you react or respond when your significant other doesn't do something you approve of, or you get wind of something they did? What and who influences how you choose to respond? Is your girlfriend hyping you up? Your mom? Songs that sing about busting the windows out his car or television shows that demonstrate toxic relationships as *goals*? Whatever it is, you need to get ahead of it and be more intentional about responding differently. I'm sure we've all heard the saying, "If you do what you've always done, you will get the same results." Well, try responding differently and see what you come up with.

Even if it doesn't make things go away instantly, it should at least begin to grow you in the fruits of the spirit. This is what pleases God. Some growth is better than no growth at all. So, if you're sitting there wondering what's the point since nothing is going to change, then I urge you to *try* because honestly, what can you lose? You're obviously not getting anywhere with your usual route, so take a healthier one and become that change you desire. Now, I will admit that a different response will take you completely out of your comfort zone and may trigger resistance. BUT that's how you know you are on the right path. The resistance is just your flesh and pride trying to stunt your growth — don't let it.

> *"Watch and pray that you may not enter into temptation. The spirit indeed is willing, but the flesh is weak"* (Matthew 26:41 ESV).

When you need to have those tough conversations with your spouse, take them to yourself before indirectly involving bystanders and nosey neighbors. More importantly, before you end up cutting your spouse with your words, try writing out what needs to be said or what you want to say, to yourself first. Then, read it back to yourself. Why? Because it allows you to see and hear the viciousness of your sword (tongue) before you go attacking someone with it. This can also be helpful in our relationships with family members, friends, or co-workers.

Then, picture your significant other coming to you with those same fiery words. Would you feel inclined to listen? Why is it that our spouse should come to us *correct* but we come to them any kind of way? Your man doesn't have to put up with that. He may do it for a while because he loves you, but eventually, that clap back gets old, sis, and he won't do it for much longer. If he allows it for the long haul, chances are he is just tolerating you (which is detrimental to your relationship). Or you just may end up with a weaker man than what you feel you started with because all those years of belittling and attacking him with your words WILL create a yes man or a silent man.

THEN, you'll find yourself complaining even MORE, not realizing that all the time you spent yelling at him and telling him everything he's not and how you could do better, could have been better spent with you loving, respecting, and building him up. No, we're not responsible for *raising* a man, but building him up is not a *motherly* thing. Just like compliments make you feel good and confident, it's the same with him. Just surviving off of *good sex* won't cut it. If we put more mindfulness into how we treat our spouse, just maybe we would see better results instead of our marriages hitting a hard place. But instead, we're tired and burnt out from playing a role we were never meant to play, which is *acting* like his mother instead of his woman: "Go do this, go do that, why didn't you take out the trash? Didn't I tell you?" It can go on, but the point is we need to leave the *nagging* to his mother.

Now, we're even more upset because we crave attention that he's no longer giving, feeling like the lack of affection happened *out of nowhere*. However, the truth is, he's been off that page for longer than we realize.We missed it because we were too focused on what we wanted and what he should've done, oblivious to the sharpness of our tongue and things we SHOULDN'T have said to him.

Some of you may still be on the fence or completely on the other side of the field on submission. You claim to submit to no one and nothing, but I beg to differ. Although your heart is in a state of rebellion at home towards your husband, why is it that you submit to, honor, and respect that male co-worker at your job more than your own husband? Could it be that you're intrigued by what he seems to present and that he appears to be *better* and less stressful than the man you have at home? Guess what? You only see one side of him and you're only mesmerized by the level of authority and power he *appears* to have. It's all smokey mirrors.

Completely ignoring this fact, you jump through hoops at work for this man with the hope of satisfying your curiosity or getting the attention you're not getting at home. You may tell yourself, "If only my husband were more like him, I would be so much more satisfied." Truth is, there could be a woman in your man's life who he thinks the same thing about as well. However, you don't give much thought to that because you think, "If they only knew what he's like, they wouldn't want him," even going to the extent of saying, "She can have him!" Don't get on your high horse assuming no one wants your husband just because of the flaws you've seen in him. The same can be said about you. Rebellious woman, you are NOT a *prize*.

Don't fall into the traps the devil has set up for you or those you may even set up for yourself as an excuse to make an exit or an *oops* in your marriage. Buddy at work just wants to get in your pants and move to the next one. He wants to invite you to go along with the illusion that he cares for you, tell you how you deserve so much better and sweet talk you right out of your senses, thereby causing you to feel you married the wrong person, commit adultery and finally, ruining your marriage. That's the enemy! You didn't feel like you married wrong when things were all good with you and your spouse. So don't use that misconception or even delusion as an excuse to dishonor God and your husband in the name of "Maybe we weren't supposed to be married." You didn't marry wrong. You treated each other wrong and are reaping the fruit of what you planted in your marriage. Both of you have some work to do. God wouldn't have you cheat on your spouse. And in case you were wondering, having sex with another person while being separated and filing for a divorce counts too. Sex outside of marriage is STILL a sin contrary to current popular belief.

God does not condone adultery or rebellion and the grass isn't greener on the other side. It's a cliché, but it's so true. When you begin to take the time to care for your garden, when you fertilize and persistently water it, you will see amazing results. Growth never prevails where persistence fails, so what's it going to be, sis? Are you going to keep leaving weeds in your garden just because it's getting a little hot outside? Are you going to keep running to your girlfriends, parents, and co-workers, telling them how horrible your relationship is? Or are you going to finally examine yourself, implement the needed changes on your end and develop a better way of responding to your spouse? It's your choice and you can't say it didn't work if you didn't give it your all. Take him off of your "He has until this date to get right or I'm out" calendar and **put yourself on it**.

Can you imagine if God treated us like that? We wouldn't be able to bear God having NO grace with us! I praise and thank God for His grace! Being that our marriages are supposed to reflect God, we need to extend His level of grace to our spouses— and even ourselves — because I acknowledge there are many times when we come to our wits' end and just can't take it anymore. However, when the going gets tough and you feel like you can't, God will give you the strength to see it through. He created marriage and wants to see your marriage succeed. If you feel like no one, including your spouse, wants to see your marriage last, trust me when I say God does. With Him, you have already won the battle.

If God is for us, who can be against us? (Romans 8:31 NKJV).

What therefore God hath joined together, let not man put asunder (Matthew 19:6 ASV).

Each time He said, "My grace is all you need. My power works best in weakness. So now I am glad to boast about my weaknesses, so that the power of Christ can work through me" (2 Corinthians 12:9).

4

Girl Bye

I want to take a self-check pause and let you know that I'm aware that the title of this book alone may be triggering or even *offensive* to some. When the Lord gave me this book to write, I felt unqualified to do so. Not only because I wasn't married at the time, but because I didn't think women who are *seasoned* counselors or married longer than me would receive it well. However, the more I wrote and the more I sought God about it, the more He revealed that it was never about me being married. It was about the false idea I had about submission that would hinder my journey in marriage if left unaddressed and uncorrected. Today, the same false idea discussed in this book is hindering many women in their marriages.

Not only did I feel unqualified to author this book, I also began to wonder how many nasty reviews it would draw, or the reception I, as an individual, would receive. I had to constantly remind myself that God put this book in me and that whatever comes from it will be for His glory. Good, bad, and indifferent, I'm just a vessel. This book was needed to help correct the negative narrative of *men* leading and women submitting, helping to bring it into perspective in order to redirect it back to its original purpose and plan. Submission is not a curse word and we should stop treating it as such. Society has a great hand in the many false narratives which have normalized the notion of a man not being the head of a household. But we're the ones to blame if we don't correct this narrative starting within our homes.

We commonly associate the word "burden" with something stressful, negative, or painful. However, spiritually speaking, a burden is also known as carrying the heart of God for something, caring for the things He cares about, and allowing our hearts to break for the things that break His. A God-given burden is an unshakeable charge to submit to the things of God and complete our assignment(s) with due diligence. This burden and charge does not end where or when we want it to; it's in everything we do until He says it's complete. Burdens that come with everyday life are secondary to the burdens God gives us.

As I will discuss in the Submission chapter, husbands have the burden to love their wives as themselves, lead their family with reverence to the Father, and seek the Lord. Wives have the burden to submit to their husband as unto the Lord, respect and honor him. Ephesians 5 is the burden and charge God has given marriages. The way we obey this command has everything to do with how we perceive our spouse and whether we even understand and RESPECT God's purpose for the way we are supposed to conduct ourselves in our marriage. With this understanding and as God's children, submission should be viewed a little differently for us in a good way.

I don't have the capacity to effectively *get the men together* because I'm not a man. If the Lord places it in me to do that, then I will. For now, I want to help my sisters in Christ to see things from a different perspective on how they should biblically handle their marriage. Even though this book is coming from a heartfelt place, it is also designed to convict, challenge, and change relationships as you know them and to provoke the needed changes. All of these should be done in love. I've seen firsthand how rebellion has impacted the men in my life and turned good men away or ended marriages. But I've never seen those women change or take responsibility for their actions still to this day, and I refuse to perpetuate that cycle. I've also seen how my pride in "You can't tell me what to do," has been taxing on myself because I was constantly fighting for my independence when no one was even trying to take it away from me.

If you're the way I was and didn't have a model of healthy, godly submission in marriage, my prayer is that this book will help you come out of that cycle. Be the light for those around you and those who will come after you. My prayer is that you will seek to understand the true definition of biblical submission and how it looks in God's eyes. My prayer is that you will have "Aha" moments while reading this book and not "Girl bye" moments. There is so much power in how we choose to respond and I want to help us respond with that power in alignment with the Word of God. I also want us to understand the gravity of how not responding in that power impacts our marriages and sets a nasty tone in our homes. I want us to understand that we don't lose power in submission. Quite the contrary, we gain it.

5

Toxic

Due to having my own share of toxicity, this may be one of the most transparent chapters of this book. I have encountered those who were toxic, been the one to try to *fix* the toxicity in others, and was ironically in denial of my own toxic ways. No matter what side you find yourself on, all positions are very dangerous. Toxic people can't do anything but spread their toxins to others. Toxicity stains, breaks, and bruises any and everything it touches. When you're a toxic person, you repeat cycles and trick yourself into believing that everyone else is the problem and not you. You believe that, if only people didn't do this or that, then you wouldn't have to respond the way you do. "If only he wouldn't take five years to respond to my text, then I wouldn't have broken his phone. If only they had listened the way I wanted them to listen, I wouldn't have exploded."

But the truth is, people are not in control or responsible for how you react. You alone decide to either keep your composure or allow your triggers to get the better of you.

From experience, toxic people dislike being alone, especially when they end up being alone because those around them get fed up with their toxic ways and walked out. It's the defining moment when someone finally walks out on you because that one *last* explosion you had was their breaking point. And right before they leave, they hit you with a gut punch statement like, "You need help." I've had moments like this that should've been an eye-opener for me to take some time to reflect and correct my behavior. Instead, I filled the void with other things because I hated being alone. I didn't want to deal with who I really was when no one was around. Neither did I want to deal with the voices of those who had pointed out the flaws in my character I strongly ignored or disagreed with. I felt that being around people or staying busy gave me an escape from thinking about all the things that were inwardly wrong or broken in me.

You see, being around people served as a distraction from all the things I would deny in public but knew were well and alive in private. The reality is, when you're alone, you can't escape the denial you usually try to avoid by getting into another relationship or inserting yourself into other people's problems. When you're alone, it all comes to life and it's in your face. In these moments, you have two choices; face it and change, OR continue to believe it's everyone else's fault and remain the same. But please take heed of this; if everyone is saying it, sis, then there is a strong possibility that there is some truth to it. You owe it to yourself to be whole and it starts by facing the truth about you and implementing a serious change.

One of the scariest things about being toxic is not being aware of it. For many years, I repeated cycles of relationships that consisted of the same things over and over again; physical and verbal abuse, lies, unhealthy dependency, and insecurity. And after each relationship, the baggage just got bigger and bigger. I never gave myself the proper time to heal and evaluate what it was about me that kept me going into the same kinds of relationships or what I was doing that they all ended the same. I would just go to the next relationship thinking it would be *different*. I never saw myself as the issue. If I'm honest, my mouth and attitude caused a lot of *trouble* in relationships. I would say the harshest things out of pain, and most of the time, it resulted in a physical altercation or something being broken or thrown. Things escalated quickly because I was never the type of person to let someone take me for granted or have someone talk to me however they wanted.

Growing up, I was always told that I had a lot of fire for someone so small. I say that not to boast but to give you a better picture of my temperament because, if mine can be calmed, so can yours. No matter how big or tall my partner was, I refused to be moved or threatened and gave it my all when I had to *defend* myself. After a while, I would go into new relationships and **purposely** say things that had typically triggered physical altercations in my **past** relationships just to see if this person would react the same way. I know it sounds crazy, but this was a safety test for me. I wanted to know ahead of time how far my words could go because I was tired of the seemingly nice guys in the beginning and then getting surprised with physicality later. The truth is, my behavior **AND** mindset were toxic, dangerous, and senseless.

So, even when my relationships ended physically, they still existed emotionally, all because I never healed or gave myself the time to. I just carried all that anger, distrust, and blame right into the next relationship, charging the new person with the negative experiences of the last. I automatically went into a new relationship mentally and emotionally toxic, broken, and disabling. At the first sign of any anger, a new guy showed, I would mentally measure him up and tell myself what I needed to do and how fast, just in case he tried to put his hands on me.

Isn't that insane??? Who wants to be in a relationship like that, let alone be WITH someone whose mind is operating that way? It's not healthy and it shouldn't be desirable OR tolerated. Period. I don't care how nice the person seems at first and how sweet they are, don't ignore those red flags. You cannot heal them. You cannot change them. That's not your job. More importantly, you're not their first rodeo and they already know how the story goes.

None of my past relationships could have helped me. Only the Lord and my willingness to change could have implemented the change. So, save yourself from unnecessary stress and let them heal. Also, you don't need to keep tabs on their progress either. No matter how much you think *checking in* helps, they may still have feelings for you and it will mislead them and possibly interrupt their healing process. If you're the one that's always triggered or brings the toxicity, go unpack your bags at the Lord's feet and let Him heal you. Don't try to rush your healing by tricking yourself into thinking you're *okay*, all because you don't want to be alone. You need that alone time. Loving will be so much more enjoyable when you're better and whole. You'll be able to love better as well as *receive* love better with no hindrance of baggage or fear. That was one of my issues. I didn't know how to receive love well and I had to dig deep to find out why. I found that it had a lot to do with my childhood and household environment in my youth.

When Joseph and I first met, I still had baggage. A LOT of it; baggage I didn't even know I had until I had to face it. I would catch myself getting angry at him over the smallest things, **expecting** him to react negatively like a guy from a previous relationship did, and he never would. I thought something was wrong with him, like he was *too good to be true*.

Completely displaced expectations!! One day, I had to ask myself, "Why am I so angry? Why am I so upset? Why do I automatically think he's going to hurt me?" I realized none of this was fair to him. He was truly different from anyone I'd ever dated and he made me feel safe. I was bleeding on a good guy and when I started to see how it impacted him, it cut me to the CORE. It was one of the worse pains I'd ever felt.

Just for imagery sake, imagine constantly pushing someone and them never pushing back but instead, showing you constant patience and fighting your fire with love. Imagine running away from home on the worst terms and when you return, finding that your loved ones never locked the door and were eagerly anticipating your return. This is the kind of love and patience he demonstrated. When I *finally* accepted the fact that he had no desire to hurt me and that I was the only one pulling the trigger, I almost lost him. He basically told me, "Hey, I love you E, but if you don't get it together, I can't do this anymore. You need to fix some things and only you can fix them. We both deserve better and it's up to you to do your part in making it better."

This was a tough pill to swallow. I cringed, realizing that I was the toxic, HURT person. I never had to face myself as the problem. None of the people I dated were perfect (no one is), so I always highlighted their wrongs over mine. Even though both parties contributed, I can only speak for my part as I was responsible for the baggage I brought in. After Joseph spoke those words, it hit me that I had to come to terms with MY faults. I had to pray for God to heal and reveal areas in my life I didn't know were damaged. I cried many nights, had panic attacks and I was in a *very low* place. No one knew about this pain I bottled up. I made it my business to hide it and when I was around other people, I put on my best face. However, on the inside, I wanted to burst into tears every five seconds and couldn't wait to get back home to shut myself in my room.

One thing that you have to be very careful about when taking time alone is what voices you let echo. If you let the Lord's voice and His word echo, you will have more peace, hope, and a sound mind that will bring clarity and direction. If you let YOUR voice echo, all of your mistakes and wrongs will be AMPLIFIED and you will constantly feel like damaged goods. That mood will become the breeding ground for the enemy to come in and snatch every ounce of healing, hope, and restoration God has for you.

There is freedom from your toxicity. You just have to be willing to address it and BE addressed. When you pray, ask the Lord to show your toxic traits or ways —and He will; the good thing is, He won't leave you high and dry to deal with them on your own. He will provide you with people, resources, and most importantly, His Word to help you heal and make you new, giving you beauty for ashes. Make no mistake; there is no overnight quick fix when it comes to healing, but healing is attainable. It's a process and you will forever be GROWING. Once you are healed and free, do not lower or bend the standards of what you will and won't allow. This will only undo your healing progress and you will find yourself in a deeper rut than before.

As a social worker in child welfare, we see a similar thing happen all too often with children. When we assess the safety and well-being of a child, it is important for us to first explore what we can do to keep the family together before having to initiate a removal. However, there are many situations when a removal is required, which can be traumatic for the child. If that child is able to be reunited with their family, the child will be full of joy and excitement. Unfortunately, oftentimes the family gets comfortable again and returns to the old habits that caused their child to be taken away in the first place. This results in a *second* removal which, more often than not, is more traumatic than the first.

They are left with so many questions such as, "How did I get here again? Don't they love me? What did I do wrong?" and begin to doubt that they can ever get back to their normal again. They thought they had come so far but it wasn't too long before everything was snatched away again just because their caregiver got *comfortable.* Just like with us, the more we re-experience the same event, the more we start to doubt our ability to become or do better.

I share that to show how imperative it is to stick to *your* growth, boundaries, and awareness of your toxic roots and anger. Being aware of and even admitting our toxicity is pertinent if we want to be better people, wives, mothers, friends and sisters. We're no good to anyone if we're not good.

Proverbs 31:10-12 says, "*Who can find a virtuous and capable wife? She is more precious than rubies. Her husband can trust her, and she will greatly enrich his life. She brings him good, not harm, all the days of her life.*" When you have the time, I encourage you to read the virtuous woman chapter in the MSG version. The in-depth picture it paints is powerful. And before you say, "I don't have to be doing all that..." just try and read it with an open mind. Ask yourself how you can apply some of those characteristics to yourself if needed. I'm not asking anyone to be perfect and I definitely won't portray the false image that I exhibit those characteristics 24/7 because I don't. However, I do believe it's a good example to glean from. If we're going to follow any example, why not make it a biblical one?

The part that really stands out for me is, "*She brings him good, not harm, all the days of her life.*" What *good* are we bringing into our marriage and relationships if our toxicity is influencing our character? What good are we to anyone if we continue to blame shift instead of taking responsibility for our actions? We play an important role in the atmosphere of our homes. We can shift it no matter how our husbands or children act. We have the power to make it a peaceful place or a sorrowful one. That's a great power that is often overlooked when we stubbornly cling to the attitude of, "I'm going to say and do what I want."

A great portion of the order and functionality of our home is in our hands. What are you doing with that burden/responsibility? We can't let our emotions run the home. We set the tone and in order to set a consistent and positive one, we have to identify where we fall short and flush out any toxins. We need to define the meaning/purpose of submission our flesh identifies with as against the meaning/purpose God put in place for submission. Then we need to align ourselves with God's purpose for marriage and...apply PRESSURE by denying our flesh.

The enemy would love nothing better than for you to idolize your independence and tear down your husband and home, so you leave a generational trail of bad examples for your children and their own children. Identify what you want your actions to teach because your children are watching and they will hear what you do, not what you say.

6

The Tale of a Man - by Joseph Britto

Having a wife who serves as your teammate is invaluable so much so God saw it fit to create a helpmeet for Adam in Genesis.

> Then the Lord God said, "It is not good that the man should be alone; I will make him a helper fit for him" (Genesis 2:18 ESV).

Even in their creation, women are characterized as a "helper" or a "helpmeet." When a woman walks in this divine purpose, she has the unique ability to bring value to everything around her, including her husband. When a man understands that his wife is his teammate, not his adversary, his world begins to transform for the better. This is the way God intended it to be.

I appreciate that my wife can submit to my leadership. Put simply, it makes life easier. Each time she submits, it fuels my desire to lead her and serve her more. While I may be confident in my own abilities, my leadership is only as effective as the confidence she places in me. Sometimes, out of our own insecurity, mis-education or trauma, we base our relationships on control and power—who has it or how can I take it back?

That is not submission. Certainly, we've had moments like this where we've been so blinded that we begin to see each other as an adversary and not a teammate. This is a tactic by our real enemy, Satan. Now, when my wife and I disagree, we strive not to be disagreeable or forget whose side we're on because the true power rests in Jesus Christ.

Two things make it difficult to lead a wife and a home; distrust and ego. That goes for both the husband and the wife. You may be asking what I mean by that. Well, let's start with the husband. If a husband has a big ego or distrusts his wife, he may always think his way is right and will eventually shoot down everything she says. This invites rebellion and resentment in the marriage, which erodes the wife's desire to submit. Similarly, if the wife has a big ego or distrusts her husband, she won't allow him to step up, be a man, and lead. Or, if he does, she will provide resistance at every turn, which then leads to nothing but confusion and frustration.

Shortly after we got married, we had a moment like this where we both let our egos get in the way. Due to finances and with COVID-19 arriving on the scene, we decided to postpone our honeymoon. While we had just enough money to take the trip, we both agreed postponing it was the safest bet. Our disagreement, however, was centered on when we should reschedule the trip. Eliyah's desire was to travel over the summer during our sixth month anniversary because she wanted to be intentional about not leaving the trip for too long. Meanwhile, I thought the most important priority was to fulfill our aspiration of homeownership, especially with our apartment lease ending in a few months. As a result, I pushed to wait another year to honeymoon. In this moment, I encountered a great deal of resistance from my bride. Days passed on and moments remained tensed as she was furious with me. She questioned my ability to lead and I questioned her thought process in return.

Later on, what we realized was that we both were right; however, our approach was wrong. On one hand, I could have done a better job at including my wife in the decision to ensure she felt heard. On the other hand, I felt she could have trusted my guidance more and not questioned my ability or intentions. As a separate note, I would also caution couples to pray against spiritual attacks in advance for when the enemy tries to cause division in your marriage. This experience served as a teaching moment for both of us because we then understood that compromise, humility, and trust are essential to submission. *"Pride goes before destruction, and a haughty spirit before a fall"* (Proverbs 16:18 ESV).

Similarly, two things make it easy for a man to lead his wife and household; respect and trust. In this context, these two things are one and the same. I will explain why. Just as women need to be loved by their husbands, men need to be respected by their wives as well. Now, both of these are reciprocal. I'm not saying only men need respect and only women need love. However, for a man to operate within his purpose as a leader to his wife, he NEEDS to *feel* respected.

This feeling is rooted in how a man views himself. For most men, we see ourselves as providers, protectors, problem solvers, and leaders for those who we love. As a result, we will act on our instincts by having an innate desire to put food on the table, protecting our loved ones from harm, and offering solutions, even if our wives only seek a listening ear, and not our opinions, after a hard day at work. When a man feels respected by his wife in these areas, what he ACTUALLY hears is, **"Honey, I trust you."** In addition to his potential to do the things stated above, these words help build him up, develop his confidence, and increase his motivation rather than chipping away at it. It is important to encourage your husband on his *journey* towards becoming a better leader.

When a man doesn't feel respected in these areas or he continually encounters resistance, he may feel humiliated, frustrated, and even emasculated. After numerous attempts to get the respect he deserves, he may shut down; becoming cold and distant to his wife and family. This is dangerous. When a man begins to separate himself emotionally or mentally from his wife and his home, he isn't fully present in the affairs of his home or within the lives which reside there. Be careful; you don't want a divided household or a discouraged husband. As his wife, you should want him to be his fullest self and your words can play a big role in that.

As you're probably thinking, "This is all easier said than done," you're right. You may be having some of these thoughts: "What if he fails me over and over; what if his job doesn't pay enough to put food on the table; what if he believes that I should be the primary one taking care of the house since I am a woman?" These are all valid concerns. Please remember that I am not saying **not to** have those conversations. What I am saying is that your choice of words has the potential to help or hurt your husband and the situation as a whole.

One thing my wife and I have implemented during disagreements is using "I" versus "You" centered statements. This was a tool we picked up during pre-marital counseling and it has helped us resolve disagreements without becoming the fire-breathing dragons we've been guilty of in the past. When you're mad, words can slip out, which can cause irreversible damage. So, maybe this technique might work for you. Try it, rather than saying, "**You** need to get up and do this" or "**You** still haven't done that," maybe you can try saying, "**I** don't feel like I am receiving enough help and this makes me overwhelmed. I need some help." Perhaps, another strategy works better for you and that's fine. The point I want to underscore is that words grow feet, so we always need to be mindful of what we say.

Prayer is a powerful tool and I want to express the importance of praying for your spouse and your marriage continuously.

In closing, for a man to lead his wife and family effectively, I believe the following three factors are essential. Leading with God's will; leading with love; and leading by example.

> For the husband is the head of the wife as Christ is the head of the church... (Ephesians 5:23).

As we can see in Ephesians, Paul compares the relationship between a husband and his wife with that of Christ and the church. We know that Jesus would never do something outside of the will of His Father. In fact, He routinely submitted to the will of His Father, including making the ultimate sacrifice for us. Therefore, God wants the best for us as His children and He has a plan for our lives. As godly leaders within their homes, men must understand and respect this fact, and be in tune with the will of God, so they know how to lead their family well.

Next, men must lead with love. I've learned from experience that the best style of leadership IS NOT being authoritative and demanding. In some situations, being firm is needed. However, relying solely on this style and having a one-dimensional view of leadership can lead to resentment and rebellion within your home. If you want to win your wife over, it must be done in love. Women will multiply whatever they are given. Our wives value being loved, led, included, and empowered. As a result, men must learn to navigate away from the drill sergeant mentality to maintain peace and order within the home. Love your wife well and she'll be more than willing to do whatever you ask.

Finally, men must lead by example. Nobody is perfect and sometimes we slip up. However, the goal is to always be intentional about walking according to God's ways and typifying His behavior to the world. Jesus Christ is the quintessential example of biblical manhood. As a result, men must look no further than Him. When a man's wife and family are watching him, it's his responsibility to set the tone! They will be representative of him, so he needs to make sure that he is serving as a good model. I want to thank my lovely wife for inviting me to this discussion. Also, I'd like to declare publicly with a resounding yes that I am proud of her, including her growth, which she has chosen to share throughout this book with the hope of inspiring others.

All the best! Men, continue to accept responsibility, reject passivity, lead courageously, and invest eternally.

7

Submission

There is nothing more powerful than a woman who knows her strength but makes the intentional decision to relinquish it. Her dignity and worth is not in clapping back and her confidence comes from a Supernatural power. Her tongue can cut hearts but she's developed herself to edify and command the room with her presence instead. She knows where her source is and rests in Him. You may try her but your failed attempts to ruffle her feathers cause her wings to unfold. She flies away with grace and dignity; leaving you to the likes of fools. There's much power in her tongue but even more in her relinquished silence. - Eliyah Britto

"Relinquish" means to "voluntarily cease to keep or claim;" "to give up." The key word is *voluntarily*, which basically means, I don't have to but I CHOOSE to. There is so much power in what you choose to do in your marriage, what you choose to say, and how you choose to react.

Submission in our carnal minds makes many of us cringe or raise an eyebrow. Society tells us that submission is a thing of the past and that it interferes with us being *a boss*. Well, how can the world define something it didn't create? It can't. Biblical submission is rooted in God alone. It has nothing to do with you. Submission is the representation of how Christ operates, which is through order as seen throughout Scripture. Things never go right where rebellion and pride reign. Biblical submission, the real submission, is a **life** representation of our relationship with Christ and His relationship with God the Father. Christ is the head of the Church (us) and God is the head of Christ. The Church submits to Christ as Christ submits to God.

Since husbands are the head of their wives and Christ is the head of the husband, we submit to our husbands, as our husbands submit to Christ, as Christ submits to God. I know that's a mouthful but this is the breakdown of the order God created. Without this order, there can be no order, only chaos. If we find ourselves having a hard time submitting to our husbands, we have to evaluate if we are submitting ourselves to the Lord. Now, before I go any further, I understand there are some people who have an unsaved spouse. In no way am I condemning you, nor am I encouraging you to run to the divorce court. I do encourage you, however, to cover your spouse in prayer and intercede on his behalf. Pray for him to be saved, to hear God's voice, to submit to God, to love you as Christ loves the Church, or whatever it may be.

Take it into prayer; be of good courage and wait on the Lord (Psalm 27:14), for He will renew your strength (Isaiah 40:31) and give you the grace you need to be your husband's helpmeet, even if he isn't submitted to the Lord just yet. I say "just yet" intentionally because I'm believing for his salvation with you and I believe God can and will do it. He can soften any heart. Just don't let yours get hardened in the waiting process. I know it's easier said than done. However, I also know, God got you: 1 Peter 3:1 says, *"Then, even if some refuse to obey the Good News, your godly lives will speak to them without any words. They will be won over by observing your pure and reverent lives."* Pray the Word back to God and watch how He works. He is faithful to perform it.

If you're single, dating, or engaged at the time of reading this book, be very aware of who you choose or are choosing. If he's not saved now but you're hoping you can change him, or he promised he would go to church with you more once you're married, etc., don't bank on that. A person who doesn't have a solid foundation in Christ has no loyalty to Christ. If you upset him or you both get into an argument on Saturday night, he may not show up for church on Sunday because he was only going for your sake and doesn't know that his identity is rooted in Christ, not on whether or not he's on good terms with you. However, when you choose someone whose identity and foundation is in Christ, he may not sit next to you at church that Sunday but he's going to go anyway because he knows his identity and his relationship with God should never change, even if his relationship with you does.

No person should be able to cause you to get angry to the extent of you not giving God the praise He deserves. If that happens, that person's *everything* is in you and not in Christ. That displaced foundation is not healthy or godly and needs to be broken now. Relationships should bring you closer to God and never make you feel guilty for doing or choosing the things of God. You don't want to spend the rest of your life dragging someone to Christ. You will experience burn out and as a result, your relationship with God will take a back seat —and God is second to no one. So, make that hard decision and let it go. It may hurt now but it will be worth it later. Marriages encounter a lot of challenges as it is, but when both are on the same page spiritually, you avoid a lot of unnecessary stress and can put your focus on other areas.

You have the wrong idea if you think biblical submission means someone is taking something away from you and is depriving you of your voice or your right to speak your mind. You and your husband are on ONE team. If one wins, you both win. When submission is in the right order, your husband values your input; hence the word HELPmeet and most importantly, values YOU. So, he wouldn't dare belittle you or make you feel your voice has no ground. Sometimes a greater yield may be needed from our end in situations where he makes a final decision. I say "greater yield" because we may not always like his final decision but we must learn how to not be offended by it, or let it interfere with our *bed peace*. Letting him have the final say does not mean he's right. It means you understand that since he is the head, the outcome of his decision will be his responsibility.

Have you ever had a friend who came to you for advice or needed help making a decision and they did the opposite of what you advised? Then you wondered why they even came to you in the first place? Well, that happens in marriages too. On BOTH sides. I can't put it all on the men. Come on ladies, even with the simplest things, we ask our husbands what they think about a certain outfit or hairstyle and then we come back with something totally different. But somehow, it's more serious when it comes to household decisions. I agree it's different but the principle is the same. We take our input seriously and just because someone else didn't go with what we said, does not mean they don't value your opinion or lack respect for you. But oftentimes, we tend to feel that way 100 percent!

However, we have to look at their heart and ask why they chose the decision they made. The best way to find out is by ASKING. Yes, ask! Don't come to conclusions and assumptions in your mind because we already know what that leads to; arguments and division. We are fighting for unity in our marriages, not division. So, don't let your *feelings* give leeway for the enemy to run rampant in your marriage.

When Joseph and I were looking for a new home, he decided to withdraw our interest on a new build community we were interested in. This wasn't just any community. This is the community I would drive past Monday through Friday on my way to work, praying about it and speaking to it as I passed, declaring that there was land with our name on it there. We joined the VIP mailing list so we could be one of the first to know about their prices and pre-grand opening. When the pre-grand opening came, I went in with so much excitement and expectancy. We toured the different models and saw the prices for each and of course, the prices increased with each square foot.

There was only ONE model that was in our price range and we both knew it would not be a home suitable for us to live in five to ten years from now. It was a house we knew we would grow out of before we even put a dent in the mortgage. So, we went to the next model up, which had everything we wanted and more, minus the price. I remembered every prayer and declaration I had made over this community and I was not going to give up so easily. Period! I was going to stretch my faith and my hands to claim what was mine. So, after touring the models, I walked us over to the appointment center and made an appointment. If I can pause right there and have you reflect on the last few words, there was a lot of *me* and *I* in there. "I walked us over." Where was I consulting my husband in any of this? I wasn't wrong for believing and having faith but I didn't fully include my husband in it. He saw my passion for this place and knew I prayed for it, so he let me exercise that, not wanting to rain on my parade. However, I dropped the ball by not seeing where his mind and desires were.

So, I made the appointment and when we got to the car, he told me that the model we knew we would grow out of was more realistic for our budget and could be done comfortably. The model that was more spacious would be pushing it and be tight. I heard him in that moment but I wasn't listening. It was like, "Yea babe, I know what it looks like, but I'm believing otherwise." I wasn't submitted to his wisdom in that moment or, to anything he said that wasn't in alignment with what I was *faithing* for. To be completely transparent, I didn't want to hear it. I told him what I was believing for and that was that.

When the reminder email came about the appointment I had so *confidently* scheduled, Joseph made the **decision** to cancel our appointment and withdraw our interest. That's not even what upset me. What upset me the most was that he didn't even tell me he was going to say what he said or do what he did and I found out via the email he cc'd me on!! So, you can imagine how I was feeling and how hard my neck turned to the side when the email popped up on my phone! Whew chile! So, what did I do? I was most definitely upset in that moment. But instead of going straight in with a confrontational spirit like I *wanted* to, I took a minute to get my thoughts, words and emotions together.

Once I knew I was able to approach the situation with a sound mind, I ASKED him why he didn't let me know he was going to withdraw our interest. He said, "Babe, I did let you know, you just weren't listening."

"What?! Excuse me? First of all..." this is what I was saying on the inside but, I CHOSE to respond with, "Okay. When did WE explicitly decide we were going to withdraw our interest?"

He said, "You're right, babe, WE didn't explicitly decide. I made the final decision because I'm not going to allow us to make decisions that will hinder our financial growth. If that is for us, God will show us but I don't have peace about us making that decision. So, as your husband, I'm not leading our household down that path. I'm sorry if you don't like the decision I made and I'm sorry for how I went about it but this is what's best for us."

Welp! My lips were shut in my face. He was right. I could've kept pressing my point because he made the final decision without consulting me, but I would've been even more upset if, down the road, we were living paycheck to paycheck just because I wanted this house and he let us get to that point. I would have questioned his ability to lead and blamed him for any financial stress incurred and for not speaking up as *the man*.

We have to be careful of how we react when our spouse doesn't go about a thing how we want them to. We can't beat them down for not being able to make a decision or lead, then get mad when they do. Pick a side; honor through submission or rebel by not listening. Pick the household you want to live in. Resistance or unity. Only one is truly functional. One satisfies your flesh and the other satisfies the Spirit. Your choice also determines who you're living for.

You may be asking, what is submission supposed to look or feel like? I know many women have had a skewed notion of submission taught to them and because of that, they hate it and rightfully so. In light of that, I have made a list of what leadership/headship is and isn't all about. So, if you find yourself, your marriage, or relationship contrary to this, then one or both parties is missing the true meaning of submission and lacks understanding of headship. In short, leadership/headship should resemble the character of Christ and submission should resemble the love, respect, and honor we are to show Christ. This is a list I've developed through my own unlearning and learning about submission and headship. Through your own learning, you may find different things to list and I hope this helps give you a head start:

What headship is not:
- Violent
- Forceful
- Degrading
- Manipulative
- Deceiving
- Evil
- Obedience (obedience is done out of fear of punishment; submission is done out of our love for Christ)
- Abusive
- Fearful
- Controlling

What leadership/headship is:
- Patient
- Kind
- Careful
- Considerate
- Selfless
- Sacrificial
- Respectful
- Loving
- Protective

Submission is not:	Submission is:
• Rude	Selfless
• Disrespectful	Loving
• Disregarding	Understanding
• Resistant	Attentive
• Quid pro quo	Patient

If you look at Ephesians 5 in the NLT version, you will see that the section dealing with marriage is titled *Spirit Guided Relationships*. So, if there is such a thing as Spirit-guided relationships, then we should know that there are worldly-guided relationships as well. The view we choose to let guide our relationships deeply depends on our willingness to understand how the two differ and the purpose that both fulfill. A lot of times, Spirit-guided relationships are misinterpreted and misunderstood, which causes what is required in a Spirit-guided relationship to be undesired.

Ephesians 5:21-24 is one of the most misinterpreted Scriptures when it comes to breaking down the concept of submission, headship, and God's design. In fact, some people forget all about verses 25-32 and just stop at 21-24. These are the people who lack understanding of what true submission is or why God put it in place. These are the people who pick and choose scriptures for power and control. That's why it's so important to KNOW God and His Word for YOURSELF. In this way, you are not easily swayed and you can straight away identify a relationship that is not of God. It will also help you accurately apply and pray the Word over your husband, home, family, and life. It's so important for the sharpness of your discernment, so you know what you need to pray against, knowing our battles are spiritual, not against flesh and blood.

Here's a breakdown of Ephesians 5:21-27 verse by verse:

21 And further, submit to one another out of reverence for Christ. (This is the command for both the husband and wife)

*22 **For wives, this means** submit to your husbands as to the Lord.* (This is the instruction/the how to for wives).

23 For a husband is the head of his wife as Christ is the head of the church. He is the Savior of his body, the church.

24 As the church submits to Christ, so you wives should submit to your husbands in everything.

*25 **For husbands, this means** love your wives, just as Christ loved the church.* (This is the instruction/the how to for the husband). *He gave up his life for her*

26 to make her holy and clean, washed by the cleansing of God's word.

27 He did this to present her to himself as a glorious church without spot or wrinkle or any other blemish. Instead, she will be holy without fault.

28 In the same way, husbands ought to love their wives as they love their own bodies. For a man who loves his wife actually shows love for himself (emphasis added).

As you can see in the above Scripture, the command for submission is not just for wives. It is for both the husband AND the wife. However, the INSTRUCTION for submission differs for both parties; but it is an instruction nonetheless. So, for those people who cut this passage off at the instruction for the wife alone, you are wrong. For me, this passage makes it perfectly clear that God did not design marriage or submission to be a *lording* over type of thing. He designed it to represent His love and relationship with us, as His church. But for many reasons, some being due to our human nature and desire for power, God's original intent and order for marriage has been disrupted. There is a much-needed work to be done to put God's order of marriage in its proper place again and as with any change, it starts with you.

8

Displaced Submission

Some of us are operating in displaced submission. When we displace something, we cause it to be removed from its proper or ordinary position. You may cringe at the word or think it's a thing of the past; however, you still submit to *something* — believe it or not — whether it's a job, your family, or even church. When they call, you *run to* it. But when it comes to submission in your marriage, do you *run away* from it? Do you put everyone else's needs above your husband? Do you leave him to fend for himself making excuses like, "He knows I'm busy," or "I have to make sure my sis is good," and my favorite, "If I don't do it, it won't get done?"

For some reason, we feel like if we aren't the ones doing the job, then it will fail or never get accomplished. Sorry to break it to you, sis, but you are NOT that powerful. Nothing and no one needs you more than God and your husband. You can't keep serving so well in church, work, friends, family, and serve poorly at home with high expectations AND demands that your husband be more *understanding* or stop *complaining* about you not being home.

Home is your first ministry, so your husband shouldn't have to beg you to serve there. If a pastor were to serve church members well but goes home to treat his wife and children like crap, he is seen as a hypocrite and you wouldn't desire to be under that leadership anymore — well, at least I hope not. It's the same with you as a wife. You've made people your headship if you serve like crazy everything and everyone else more than your own husband. How can you submit to your pastor, the church or the needs of others better than you do your husband? I don't care who said that was okay, but I'm letting you know now, it's not and that it's not biblical.

1 Timothy 3:5 says, "*If a man cannot manage his own household, how can he take care of God's church?*" This Scripture was addressing leaders in the church. However, even if you're not a leader in the church, you are a leader somewhere and the point still stands. Take care of home *first* and well. This applies to anything or anyone that will cause you to neglect the needs of your household. No one should be able to brag about how well you serve if your own husband can't. How would you feel if your husband's friends or co-workers raved on and on about your husband's cooking, but he never cooked for you? Or if they bragged about how patient he is but he lacks patience with you? I don't know about you, but I would be hurt because as his wife, I'm supposed to have the best of him, not what's left over.

If you're the type of person people can call on to get the job done, then people have probably come up to your husband left and right, letting him know how lucky he is to have you. But he may not feel lucky after all because he's only gotten what's left over of you. Even when you come home, you complain about how tired you are and don't give him the time of day. Why should he feel *lucky*? When this happens, he is at risk of one of the greatest losses in his life: losing the woman he loves to the needs of others. When others' needs get the better of you and his needs go unnoticed or overlooked, he will begin to pull away and possibly resent the things you dedicate yourself to. He may even begin to feel insecure and frustrated as he wonders, "Why doesn't my wife serve me like that, what am I not doing, am I enough?"

He may not even express these feelings to you because, one, you already have a bad track record when it comes to responding to his needs or vulnerabilities by being dismissive or, two, he doesn't want to come off as weak or needy. You may not even be conscious of the damage that you're causing him or your marriage. Or... maybe you are aware. Maybe you purposely avoid serving your husband and overextend yourself in other areas because you're trying to avoid something that may require *the more of you* that your marriage needs. Maybe it's a child, maybe it's sex, or maybe it's simply being close and vulnerable with your spouse in having to face those very things you tried to avoid. Or maybe it's the voices of *people* who don't respect marriage, convincing you that your husband needs to *man up* and is wrong for wanting the more of you.

The movie, *Deliver us From Eva* is a great example of displaced submission. All of Eva's sisters were married or in a committed relationship, but they were submitted to her and not their spouses. Anything she advised or didn't like, they submitted to. They would even subject themselves to her teachings, then bring back her rulings to their homes. "Eva says this or Eva says that, so we should do it." The division and burden this caused in their relationships were evident to the viewers, but not to the sisters. What Eva said was Bible and they didn't stray from it.

I'm sharing this example to draw a picture of what allowing outside voices into your home can do to your marriage. Don't let the opinions of your family or friends run your marriage. If you do, I guarantee you that they will ruin it. Whatever the reason is for your avoidance, it is imperative that you get to the bottom of it. If you don't, you are missing out on the amazing opportunity to live out a Kingdom marriage that God wants for you. You never know, the thing you're trying to avoid or struggling with in your marriage can be the very thing God wants to use to help heal someone else's marriage. Too many people think they're alone in what they're going through — and that's just not true. The Bible tells us that we overcome by the blood of the lamb and the word of our testimony, so, testify sis.

When we submit to the thoughts of highly opinionated family members, friends, this world and even unsound preachers, we miss our opportunity to get out of hindering cycles of comfort. I remember when Joseph and I first got engaged, I told a family member that I would be leaving our home church to join his church. This was a hard decision for me because I love my church. I knew everyone and I just never saw myself leaving. She responded with, "Don't let no man take you away from your church. The man is supposed to leave his church and come to the woman's church." Huh?? I know a man is supposed to leave his family and cleave to his wife. But leave his church? That's definitely not biblical. Because I know the Word for myself and sought God about it, I knew He had given me the green light, so her opinion did not make me waver or cause me to go back to Joseph with "She said, he said."

So, not only is it important to know the Word for yourself and to hear from God, but it's equally important to be proactive about not entertaining foolish conversations about your spouse or marriage. It's one thing for someone to pull you to the side out of concern, but it's another thing when someone is speaking from their own hurt, thereby projecting their outcome on you. And when it comes to seeking counsel about your marriage, it should be wise counsel and your ability to discern whether their spirit, or any spirit for that matter, is of God, should be on 100.

Unwise counsel will tell you things like, "He can fix his own plate," or "You don't have to tell him where you're going." Wise counsel will tell you when you're doing too much and that you should take care of your home FIRST. We can't be so busy trying to be superwomen for the world, while our homes are deserted. When you come home, I bet you want and *expect* dishes washed, beds made, clean floors, pee off the seat, socks in the hamper etc., because you're too tired to do anything else. I get it. However, what happened to the importance of your husband's expectations of you? Or do they not matter anymore? You have to respect him just as much as you want him to respect you. You wouldn't want him avoiding spending time with you or giving everyone else his time and leaving you out to dry. What example are you showing your children, or even those you displace your submission to? Or do you have them thinking you take care of home just as much, if not better than you do their needs? You can front if you want, but the truth comes out.

Furthermore, if people are knowingly letting you neglect your husband, while seeing you serve in extraordinary ways for them, you don't need those people in your corner or team. You need to have people who honor and respect your marriage enough to tell you to *go home*. If it's a job, start working your true eight-hour shift and stop putting in overtime for an employer who will have your positions filled within weeks, or even days of your absence. If it's church, stop overworking yourself and excusing it as the work of the Lord. No sis, God isn't in the neglecting business. When He blessed you with your spouse, He expected you to steward your part in the marriage well. He's not interested in all the wonderful things you're doing in the community if you have done NOTHING, or the bare minimum, for the union He brought you to. Home is where it all starts.

9

Bed Peace

You probably can guess from the title what this chapter is about, and you're probably right. It's about that three-letter word: sex. Yes, SEX! If that made you uncomfortable reading it, it's okay. I was a little uncomfortable typing it, but it's all good! We should never feel ashamed of what God created. Society has made sex more explicit than what it should be, and the church has made it more taboo than it should be. The reality is, God created it for a beautiful purpose within the bounds of marriage.

Now, why are we discussing sex? Because I want to shed some light on how some of us use sex as a *quid pro quo* tactic on our spouses. "If you do this for me, then I will give you that, or if you don't do this, then I'm not giving you *none.*" And that's just not how God created it to be. It's imperative that we do not use our anatomy in a conniving way. Like it or not, there is always someone not too far from your husband who is ready and willing to give him full access to her body without him having to ask or beg for it.

I want to make it crystal clear that having intercourse with your spouse should never be out of fear of him cheating. And I do not agree that men or women should step out of their marriage either. The point I want to make is that sex inside of marriage is sacred. It should not be treated as a *treat* that's kept in a box, and can only be accessed on *good* behavior. When you said yes at the aisle, your body was no longer just yours, and the same goes for your husband. You two are now *one*, according to Ephesians 5:31. The Bible also makes it clear that we should only deny our spouse sex under one condition, which is if both parties agree so that you both can give yourselves more time in prayer. And even then, the Bible advises it to be for a *limited* time.

> *The husband should fulfill his wife's sexual needs, and the wife should fulfill her husband's needs. The wife gives authority over her body to her husband, and the husband gives authority over his body to his wife. Do not deprive each other of sexual relations unless you both agree to refrain from sexual intimacy for a limited time so you can give yourselves more completely to prayer. Afterward, you should come together again so that satan won't be able to tempt you because of your lack of self-control* (1 Corinthians 7:3-5).

Yes, I know some of us get upset very often by our spouses—I get it; but going back to some of the previous chapters, we have to dig deep and find out why we are *always* upset with our spouse and why we may lack patience with him. Some of us even get irritated if our spouse breathes too hard. What is the ROOT cause of that irritation towards him? Could it be him not having a good job, not making enough money, the fact that you desire him to be someone he's not—comparing him to another woman's husband? When we deal with that root, we unlock the keys to our individual peace and happiness and most of all, we unlock the keys to a better marriage.

This may raise some eyebrows, but your happiness is not your husband's responsibility: it's yours. If you wait on him to make you happy, you will never be happy. Why? Because he's human just like you, and will *fail* you as you will fail him also. I'm not talking about infidelity, rather I'm talking about the simple things. He may not remember to bring you flowers, he may not text back quick enough or he may forget to take the trash out. You may forget to pick up the pizza for his guy's night, or to pick up his shirts from the Cleaners. Whatever it is, your happiness cannot be dependent upon his actions or the lack thereof. Only God is unfailing and because of that and the fact that we are to be more like Him, we must extend the same grace that God gives to us when we fail Him, to our spouse. Happiness starts within, and what we allow to infiltrate, that is on us.

There can never be bed peace if there is no relational peace. If that's the case, it screams toxicity. The only way you can strongly dislike someone, argue with them day in and day out and only come together for sex, is in a toxic and dysfunctional relationship that's most likely rooted in lust. Hebrews 13:4 tells us that marriage should be honored and that the marriage bed is undefiled. Now, in this context, Paul was referring to adultery defiling the marriage bed. However, I'm going to take it a step further and say that our attitudes, words, and actions can also defile our marriage beds if they are causing a hindrance to intimacy with our spouse.

We can agree that anything done outside of the will of God is considered sinful, right? Well, if our attitudes, words and actions are hindering us from having sex with our husbands — which pleases God — then we may be committing sin and aren't even aware of it, while brushing it off because it doesn't seem like a *big deal*. Well, it's a big deal to God. He doesn't want you or your spouse to fall into temptation. He especially doesn't want you to cause your spouse to fall into temptation because you make it difficult to be intimate with you. Your husband is your teammate. No team who wants to win will use bribery on their teammate (the cookie jar mentality), or sabotage their win by giving the opposing team the plays. Instead, they make a plan and work to accomplish it. *Together*. That's how we should view our marriage. One team, one goal, and one win, instead of putting him on the sideline just because he didn't make a touchdown.

You might be saying, "I'm not going to have sex with someone who upset me." My question to that is, what role are you playing in reconciling? Are you the one making the effort or are you the one rejecting his efforts? Start there to determine what changes need to be implemented. Choosing to stay angry isn't the best move. With listening, comes understanding, and with understanding, comes better responses. Once we understand why our spouse may do something or act in an unfamiliar way, our response to it should change. This doesn't mean we condone what they may say or do, but we take out our part in the flame which weakens the impact of the fire. Fighting fire with fire in your marriage leads to the burning of innocent things such as your job, your children, family, friends or finances. But if we make the choice not to respond the way we used to, or the way our flesh wants us to, the flames become easier to extinguish. If your spouse is breathing fire, you can choose to be the one who puts out the fire. If you choose to breathe fire back, there is no one there to do the extinguishing and you'll both be consumed by a fire created as a result of the pride you both let prevail.

If you and your spouse are struggling with intimacy issues, I would encourage you both to seek counseling. Talking about intimacy issues with your spouse may be difficult or even uncomfortable, so I know adding another person in the mix may intensify that discomfort. However, if it is something you don't believe can be worked out between the two of you, please work through that discomfort for the sake of your marriage. There are many other reasons that contribute to hindrances in our marriage bed whether it's past trauma of abuse, infidelity, rape, struggles with sexual identity, low sex drive, body image, children—the list goes on and on. Whatever your hindrance is, it's worth fighting through to see what's on the other side.

These hindrances cause walls to be built into our marital intimacy. When those walls are broken down, it creates so much more space for you and your spouse to experience intimacy on another level. If you choose to keep those walls up, they may cave in on you, thereby causing *your* happiness to be on the line and even your marriage. It will also result in pushing your spouse away and if he's not aware of your fears or struggles, he will think it's *him* and *pull* away. That is an unnecessary divide you don't need in your marriage. We face enough attacks in our marriages, so we have to be more intentional that there is no internal sabotage. I'm rooting for you and submitting this prayer for you to pray:

> *Lord, I thank You for the creation of marriage and what it represents. I thank You that You blessed me with the gift of marriage and allow my husband and me to be joined together as one. I ask that You increase our understanding of the purpose and importance of intimacy in our marriage. I ask that You open my heart to be more vulnerable with my spouse and to receive his affection (pray the same for him if needed). Help us to love and serve one another selflessly. I ask*

that You reveal any hindrances in our marriage that is causing unfulfilled intimacy and help us work through them together. I pray that You will heal any emotional stains left on our marriage bed, our hearts, and even our childhood wounds that play a role in our intimacy. Refine us for Your glory and let our marriage be pleasing in your sight. In Jesus' name, amen.

10

What Are You Willing to Do? : High Maintenance

Before our engagement, Joseph and I always loved to go look at homes in different communities in order to get a feel of what we wanted in our future home. So, when we got engaged, I thought that finding what we wanted would be a breeze. As we became more intentional about our first home search, he gave me a budget to stick to. If you're anything like me in that area or can recall the *Submission* chapter, then you can pretty much imagine how well I stayed within that! I did my best though! Anyway, I would pull up houses within the said budget, sometimes a little over, and send them to him. When it came to the homes he knew were a little over our budget, he would say, "Let's go see it and if we love it or have a peace about it, we will explore other finance options."

I would say, "Okay!" And then end up falling even more in love with the home once we saw it in person, but our search would continue just to make sure we were SURE about that home. After months of doing this, it got to a point where I got tired of *just going to see*. I wanted to actually start the process of buying our first home. I wanted to see us actually making tangible arrangements to secure our first home. It seemed like we would come to a decision on one house, talk about plans for a down payment, but when it came to our realistic numbers, he would hit me with, "It's smarter to rent with all that we have going on." Was he right? Yes. We were planning and paying for a wedding, I just finished grad school and was on the search to find a job in my field. He was in the process of changing grad programs, and we both were trying to learn how to combine our finances effectively. On top of that, I didn't want just any house; I wanted a new construction home! Me and my optimistic self, had this strong belief that we could do it all. However, in reality, I knew that waiting and renting temporarily made the most sense instead of rushing into a mortgage that would be way over our heads.

But one day, I got frustrated with us not taking any action on the houses, so I asked him, "Why keep taking me to all these houses if we're not going to live in one? No, I don't want to rent but if that's our reality for the moment, then just say that. I don't like getting my hopes up."

He looked at me, took a pause and said, "You're right. I know that I need to do a better job at managing expectations and I should have said something sooner. My goal was for us to live in a new build and it seemed achievable until I left my job. But when I saw how happy you were, I wanted to do anything to make it possible, despite what our budgets are saying. I wanted to make that possible for you and for us" (*insert tears*).

If you know my husband, then you would know that he is a hard worker, hands down. He's the type of person who gets his hands dirty in order to provide for his family, and make sure that his hands are clean before he comes home just so you don't get worried about his well-being. Just to be clear, I'm not referring to anything illegal. I'm using "hands dirty" as a figure of speech. He would rather take on the workload of two just so my hands can remain clean. This is where we clash sometimes because I'm the type of person that is willing to get right down there WITH him and get my hands dirty, too. This is also where my strong personality can come off as *rebellious* and not trusting he can handle it. So, I have learned to let him take the lead and give him the chance to let *me* know where he needs my assistance and how *we* can work together, instead of jumping out there to *get it done* just so it can be *taken care of.*

So with that, I let him know right then and there that I didn't need a *new* house if it was going to cause him to unnecessarily work his fingers to the bone. I don't need or want for much, and that's why when I do desire something, he goes to heights and depths to get it for me. But I want us to be healthy mentally, physically, emotionally, financially and spiritually before anything. A new house will come and so will other material things, but I'd rather have what we can financially afford at the moment than lose what we will have to pay for mentally, emotionally, and spiritually later.

All of this self-inflicted financial stress on our marriage could lead to a divorce or a non-peaceful home. Do you know that finance is one of the leading causes of divorce? I refuse to let that steal our marriage. His peace and our relationship are not worth financial and emotional burdens that can be avoided simply by making *smarter* financial decisions. Some material things are just not worth the risk of losing the love, partnership, and intimacy in your marriage. We have to learn how to separate our wants from our *needs* and be REAListic when it comes to our finances.

How many of us don't care what our man has to do, risk or sacrifice just to get us what we want? Are your wants or what you may claim as a need, even realistic? Do you show understanding when he says, "No, we can't afford that right now?" Or do you belittle him and boast about someone else being able to provide what he can't at the moment? When you do that, you are killing his confidence! You may not see it because their pride won't let them show it but trust me, it's damaging their confidence. When you boast about an ex, your dad, a family member or whoever is able to do this and that for you, he shrinks on the inside. You are literally taking whatever ounce of confidence he has left after he battles with the world when the world already tells him that he doesn't measure up with society's idea of success. And then he has to come home to the same thing? What are we doing to our men? Let's take a moment to reflect on how we responded negatively to a valid *no* he gave to a financial matter, and what we could've said or done differently.

Many of our actions need deep thought before we make a move, but we don't take heed to that. We want what we want, and we want it now. Now is the time to stop that unhealthy cycle of shooting first, and then asking questions later. Get clarity. With clarity comes understanding, and with understanding comes solutions, and with solutions come oneness and ultimately, peace. Also, put an end to the false idea that you need to have X number of things or money to have *made it*. Just because someone you admire on social media has it, that doesn't mean you need it. Or should I change admire for idolize? Remember, your budget works for your house and their budget works for theirs. If you desire *more*, first be faithful with what you have. Being faithful with what you have also includes not coveting what someone else has. *"His Lord said unto him, Well done, good and faithful servant; you have been faithful over a few things, I will make you ruler over many things. Enter into the joy of your lord"* (Matthew 25:23 NKJV).

If he puts you on a shopping budget, be understanding. You know his and your financial situation, so you know whether he is being *cheap* or not. If he's being realistic, stop trying to find other avenues to get what you want. Stop trying to keep up with the Joneses and do what you can with what you have. Have you ever thought that your financial freedom may be hindered due to your financial rebellion in your marriage and your bad spending habits? Many of you won't like that, but I encourage you to take a good look in the mirror and prioritize what you feel is needed. If the Lord can't trust you to submit to your husband in your finances, how can He trust you to submit to Him when He gives you an increase? It's all connected, sis.

If God told you to sow a seed into someone else's life that cost the same amount as that Balenciaga bag you want, would you hesitate? Let's be honest. Many times, we see the price tag of these *things* we want and rationalize why we would pay so much for it. But when that same price tag is on something that we actually need or that God may be asking us to sow, we hesitate or question the cost. I'm guilty of this myself, but being aware is only half the battle. We need to shift our mentality and hearts when it comes to our finances. Those material things you go to bat for or purchases you hide from your husband are costing you your marriage, and there's no amount of money that can front that bill.

Now, some of you may be reading this and are saying, "We're good over here financially, sis" and that's GREAT! However, are there any areas where you could cut back? Are there any areas where you can spend less and yield more to the Lord, your community, your family or church? What are you racking up on—red bottoms and Gucci? OR are you investing and building up the Kingdom and seeking the Lord about what to do with your *overflow*? Some of you may even cringe at that and say, "I give my tithe and donate to charity. What more do you want me to do?" Well, there's always a need in the kingdom and your community. Your wealth is not your own. The Lord gives and the Lord takes, but I strongly believe that when we continue to cling to Him and not our finances and remain obedient in *all* things, He will make sure our well never runs dry.

Don't get me wrong, there is nothing wrong with treating yourself every now and then. If you are tithing and taking care of what needs to be taken care of *first*, by all means, do your thing, but while you're at it, make sure you are continuing to build that savings, business, etc. Make sure also that your purchases aren't causing division in your house. It may be *your* money, but again remember that when you said yes at that aisle, everything between you and your spouse became one. Now, if you two have an agreement that you keep yours and he keeps his and bills are shared, then do what works for your household. However, there may be a bigger root to why you both desire to keep your finances separate. It could be trust issues, doubt of the marriage lasting, 'what if' statements about divorce —you name it. If that's the case, you may have a problem deeper than finances.

Ultimately, don't put yourself in a position where the Lord has to humble you. Be a cheerful giver and yield your wealth to the Lord without fearing lack. Listen when your husband makes sound decisions for the financial well-being of your household and marriage. It can't go with you to heaven, so don't let it be the reason you end up in the opposite direction. *"For the love of money is the root of all kinds of evil. And some people, craving money, have wandered from the true faith and pierced themselves with many sorrows"* (1 Timothy 6:10).

High Maintenance

When he has to constantly live up to your materialistic standards, especially if they are out of his means or even his character, it will most definitely affect his confidence as a man in a negative way. If he's not a flashy person or someone who is into expensive things and you continually put him down for it, it will cause him to shut down. When you guys are out with *your crowd* who echoes your taste in material things, he will constantly measure himself up to those around you and wonder why you both are even together. That actually may even be a question you want to consider asking yourself. Why are you with him if you feel like he's boring and doesn't fit in? Why are you trying to change him? Is it for the approval of family and friends? What initially attracted you to him? Is this relationship a security blanket for you or a divine connection God placed you in? Examine yourself because just as much as you wouldn't want him to change you to fit his *idea*, don't try to change him to fit yours. I'm officially firing you from the mold-a-man business, to giving him the space and freedom to be himself. Encourage and build him up instead of telling him how boring he is every five minutes. What are you doing to help him to tap into his adventurous side? Stop complaining while expecting results of substance. You knew how he was before you said *yes*. Anything he does to *fit in* is just to please you and it's eating away at him internally.

As people, we naturally respond better to acceptance and compliments versus disapproval and negative criticism. Do you understand maybe why he hasn't responded the way you want him to? Put down your social media infected idea of a man and start building yours up for who he is and watch how beautifully you help him become who God intended him to be.

11

Talk It Out

Sometimes the simplest solution to our relational issues is the thing we complicate the most: communication. We don't like to express our feelings, or we have a toxic way of doing so. Sometimes we may be great at communicating, but our spouse isn't or vice versa. This can negatively impact the way our spouse receives our grievances, or our desire to express them.

When it comes to planning, finances and the surface level things, my husband and I communicate those together very well. However, when it comes to verbalizing and expressing how the other person feels, my husband has me beat in that area. I don't say that to brag about him or downplay myself. I say that because this book is about transparency, growth, and the importance of changing negative habits in your relationship; to be better vessels for the Lord and healthier people for our marriages. I can't accomplish the purpose of this book with *phoniness*. So, even though I have come a long way with articulating my feelings in a healthy and communicable manner, it was not easy.

Personally, I used to never explicitly say how I felt. I just showed it and the individual felt it. I don't mean that in a physical sense, but in my demeanor and actions towards the person such as, the silent treatment, rolling my eyes, ignoring phone calls and text messages, or being short in my responses. By using such nonverbal signals, I was pretty much expecting the other person to know what they had done to offend or hurt me. I expected them to *read my mind* and come to me with an apology or explanation for what they did. I felt that letting my actions speak for me exempted me from the responsibility of having to explicitly say, I was hurt or I was offended because I felt that my actions were sufficient enough to send the message to the other party that they had done something wrong.

Having to verbalize what someone did to hurt me or upset me was a sign of weakness in my mind. This is certainly not a healthy mindset and that way of communicating is full of arrogance and pride. It takes humility and maturity to be able to tell someone that you're hurt by their words or actions toward you. It's one thing to say you *pissed me off*, but it's another to be able to *calmly* express what that person did and why it upset or hurt you. To be honest, a lot of us don't want to go there. We believe that when someone does something wrong they should know what they did, and should just apologize for it and work to correct it. Now, with some things that is absolutely true. I'm not talking about obvious offenses such as abuse or infidelity. That should be CLEAR to the offender that their actions resulted in harm. In those cases, it goes beyond an apology; there needs to be counseling and action plans set in place to address that.

With that being said, we cannot expect our significant other to be a mind reader. The guessing games need to stop sooner rather than later. Tell that man, in a calm way, what bothered or hurt you and why. When communicating your feelings to someone, use *I* statements and not *you* statements. My husband touched on this in Chapter 6 but I want to reiterate that it helps the person on the receiving end be more willing to hearing your side and lessens the chances of them feeling attacked or being on edge. I know it may seem exhausting, but it's true. After reading that, some of you may be saying, "Yea, tried that and it didn't work," and some of you may have experiences whereby that strategy completely turns on you and ends with the person saying, "Well, I'm not in control of your feelings, your feelings are on you" (*eye roll*).

I've encountered both and those are toxic and minimizing responses. You may even be the one to respond this way or be completely dismissive of what your spouse is bringing to you. Either way, those are responses from someone who doesn't like to take responsibility for their actions, and they are completely oblivious or in denial to the reality that they *actually* hurt someone. When you receive or give those types of responses, there's a very slim chance that they or you will change at the rate desired to see growth. It will take prayer and multiple approaches and possibly marriage counseling to get you or your spouse's point of view understood. The two of you have the right to determine what is and what isn't worth it when it comes to healing broken areas in your marriage. My prayer is that you both will decide to do what is worth it and see its fruit.

If you're married, some things to consider are:

How many times has he or I responded this way?
What triggers this dismissive response from me or my spouse?
Do I believe we can get through this?
Have I prayed about this?
Is he aware that this is an unacceptable response? Am I aware of my unacceptable responses?

What communication strategies have we tried and what were the outcomes? Why were those the outcomes?

If you're single, the things to consider are:

Is this what I want to accept for the rest of my life?
Do I communicate in a healthy way? Does he?
What baggage is hindering my ability to communicate in a healthy way?
Am I settling?
What red flags am I overlooking?

We have to choose our battles and if some things aren't worth addressing, then don't address them. Only you know what those things are in your relationship/household. If you've had to say it more than once, then it's probably not worth addressing *again*. One thing to think about is how often you have already addressed a certain issue and if anything has changed. Oftentimes, we don't see growth because we choose not to leave *that thing* alone.

When I was younger, I was a tomboy, to say the least. Always playing football outside with the boys, fighting or climbing trees and often coming home with a new cut. When my cut scabbed, I would constantly pick at it and the wound would reopen, causing it to bleed again. I remember my dad telling me, "If you keep picking at it, it won't get better. Leave it alone." This same instruction can be applied to our marriages. Don't keep picking at it. You addressed it once; now give it some time to heal/change. Set rules and boundaries for yourself when it comes to addressing issues. It will help you to keep yourself accountable to not *picking the scabs* in your marriage.

One rule I've set for **myself** to aid in better communication habits in my marriage is this: if something my husband does bothers or offends me and stays on my mind for more than two to three days, I address it. If it lasts shorter than that, I let it go because chances are, it wasn't worth addressing or wasn't a big deal. I'm not saying that this is biblical or even clinical, but it works for me. I want to share it with you in hopes that it helps to guide you to set your own communication strategies and self-boundaries. You're free to use my strategy if you like!

I also take into consideration my *hormones*. I can't speak for everyone, but for me, my emotions and sensitivity are heightened during certain times of the month. But I didn't always realize this. When I finally did, I used that to gauge whether his actions and words were really offensive or if I was taking it out of context because I was dealing with *PMS*. I used to not believe PMS impacted my emotions. I used to get angry when my husband would suggest my attitude or frustration was due to my *period*. I would blow up on him just for asking, "Are you on your period?" In response to an issue or concern I was bringing to him because it made me feel like he didn't think my feelings were real. However, I began to realize that when those same things occurred outside of my PMS window, I either brushed them off, didn't notice, or just didn't care. To be clear, my husband is very loving and considerate of how I feel and knows me to perfection. And because he knows me, he knows what usually does or doesn't bother me, so when I come to him with an issue that is out of my norm of offenses, it is usually during PMS. The fact is, he noticed that pattern before I did and called me out on it, even though I was resistant to it at first.

How many times has your spouse or a loved one called some of your negative behavior patterns out, and because you didn't see it, you weren't receptive and became resistant or angry towards them? Now, you should never allow anyone to minimize your emotions due to your anatomy. However, if you notice a pattern of behaviors or heightened emotions around certain times or seasons of your life, it's worth taking a closer look into.

Some questions to ponder are:

Are your emotions heightened around a certain time or season? What are those times/seasons?
When you revisit certain situations in your mind, were there other factors that contributed to your reaction?
Do you feel immediate guilt after you lash out on your loved one(s)? Why?
Do you know what your triggers are and the root cause of them?
Do you get defensive when someone calls you out on something? Why?

I began to realize the pattern of my negative responses to situations once I finally stopped getting on the defensive side. I never listened to what he was saying and just ascribed my attitude or temper to being a part of **me**. Wrong answer. You don't have to be ruled by your emotions and being toxic does NOT have to be in your character. Make the decision of who you will be and how you will react to your irritations today. Learn your body and learn your *triggers*. Identifying your triggers gives you the upper hand on your emotions and the ability to produce a better response when triggered.

Sometimes we want to blame others for getting us upset. But the reality is, our resistance to correction and ignorance of what gets us to the point of irritation is where we fail, leaving room for great offenses to recur in our lives. If you have never sat down and thought about your triggers, I encourage you to do that now. If you don't know where or how to start, there are many worksheets available online.

One activity that I have personally used and seen work for others is this trigger chart activity. Take a piece of paper, make four columns with the following headings:

1. Trigger— what makes you go from 0-100?
2. Current response— what is your immediate reaction?
3. How I wish to respond— what would be your ideal healthy response going forward?
4. Root of the trigger— what created this trigger? (childhood is a good place to start and work your way up to adult life)

I like this chart because not only does it help you to identify your triggers, but it gives you a bird's eye view of the various hindrances to your emotional well-being as well as the ability to get ahead of them.

Now, I understand that using PMS as a measuring tool to check our emotions may rub some people the wrong way. It used to rub me the wrong way as well. However, from personal experience, when I learned to be open to getting down to the root causes of my negative responses and got out of the resistance/offense mode, I gained the discipline and ability to identify where my *anger* was coming from.

Will you be open to identifying yours? At the end of the day, if you have truly taken the time to evaluate your emotions, why you feel that way, how often you respond in a certain way or identified your negative behavioral patterns, you will know yourself best. So, whatever the pattern or trigger is, come up with a plan and be intentional about not responding in an impulsive or your *usual* way. Like I mentioned before, when I would revisit certain conversations or situations after my PMS was over again, I did NOT feel the same way I did initially. I would think to myself, why did I react that way? It really was not that serious. Self-reflection goes a long way, especially if you can do this *before you go off.*

Questions to ask yourself:

Why is this making me upset?
Is my initial reaction linked to a deeper issue?
Am I jumping the gun because I'm expecting him to act or respond like my ex (refer to *Toxic* chapter for my personal experience with this)?
How have I contributed to the situation?

How does this burden a man? Well, if he is constantly trying to put your puzzle together, you run into a high risk of pushing him away or losing his attention completely. He will get TIRED of chasing you in order to figure out what is wrong with you. We are not little girls anymore and love is not a playground. So, we need to learn how to communicate like adults and get to the root of the issue. Right now, it may seem fine because he constantly checks on you, asks you what's wrong or what he did to upset you. You like his chase, so you don't desire to change your ways. However, when that *running after you* stops and believe me, it will surely stop, you will be wondering why *he doesn't care anymore.* He's not a fan of this chase you have him on andyou arel losing your horse in this race. Talk it out in a healthy manner. That way, you two can walk out the purpose

God has for your marriage in harmony, ready and able to fight what may come your way *together*.

> *Can two people walk together, unless they are agreed?*
> (Amos 3:3 NKJV)

> *Two people are better off than one. For they can help each other succeed. If one person falls, the other can reach out and help. But someone who falls alone is in real trouble. Likewise, two people lying close together can keep each other warm. But how can one be warm alone? A person standing alone can be attacked and defeated, but two can stand back-to-back and conquer. Three are even better, for a triple-braided cord is not easily broken* (Ecclesiastes 4:9-12).

12

Divorce

One thing I've seen that mostly damages intimacy in marriages is infidelity. When you find out that your spouse has given themselves to someone else, it can shatter your desire to give yourself to them again. Or vice versa, if you were the one to step out. Whoever did it, the impact and damage it causes can be most detrimental. It may have even led to divorce for some and sparked conversations of divorce for others. Biblically speaking, divorce is warranted in this circumstance. *"But I say that a man who divorces his wife, unless she has been unfaithful, causes her to commit adultery. And anyone who marries a divorced woman also commits adultery"* (Matthew 5:32).

I know that there are many people who divorced beyond this reason, and get married again. The question often is: are they sinning? I don't have a definitive answer for you, my opinion is only based on Scripture. But I do know that God's grace and mercy extends to us in all circumstances, and that seeking His face through prayer and fasting will help you in knowing what He is leading you to do.

If you encounter infidelity in your marriage, you have the right to divorce and you also have the right to decide to be reconciled to your spouse. The decision is up to you. I wholeheartedly believe that God can take the most painful parts of our lives and turn them into something powerful for

His Kingdom. Just because divorce is acceptable under this circumstance, doesn't mean your marriage has to end or that you're wrong for wanting to make it work. Healing can take place with the willingness of you both. Though it may not be easy, it is possible.

One thing both of these decisions have in common is that they both require forgiveness. Yup, you must forgive. You may think that not seeing the person will expedite your healing so you opt for separation or divorce, but healing is a process. You may not have to come face to face with him after the divorce, but you may come face to face with things, people or places that remind you of him often and you just can't run from the world.

Divorcing doesn't make it any less difficult and neither does staying. And just because you forgive doesn't mean you have to stay. I know this may seem like back and forth advice; however, I want to be sure I'm highlighting both options so I'm not downplaying either choice. These are real dilemmas that some may be dealing with, and I want them to know that if they decide to divorce after infidelity, they're not wrong and if they decide to stay, they're not wrong either. God can use both decisions for His glory. You may be stuck as to what to consider when making this decision, so here are a few things I think will help you with that decision:

1. Has the person repented to you and God?
2. Have they shown any meaningful positive changes in their behavior?
3. Have you both tried counseling?
4. Has this happened before? If so, is this just who the person is?
5. What led up to this?

Finding out what led up to infidelity does not condone infidelity. It allows both parties to see the error in their ways. You have every right to feel that his cheating was no excuse and was greater than anything you did. With that in mind, it also doesn't erase the fact that both sides could have done something different or better.

Though in some situations, infidelity may lead to divorce, I encourage couples to work through hard times. There are many things that can land a marriage on the rocks. For instance, many marriages split over money disagreements, varying spiritual views, domestic violence, mothers-in-law, in-laws in general and more. Despite this reality and state of our marriages today, we can find hope in knowing that many couples have withstood the fire and found ways to love, communicate, and grow through the pain. Divorce should never be the first resort. Resources such as prayer, counseling, couples' therapy, and marriage retreats should be considered. As long as you're still married, it's never too late to work on your issues and face them head-on. Don't brush problems under the rug or run away from the things that are eating away at your marriage. Confront these issues, communicate, and fight for your marriage. Here's a look at what happens when it is too late. I would like to illustrate a vignette that will call for your imaginative skills. As you read, keep these questions in mind:

> Where did Kendra miss the mark?
> Where did Jeremiah miss the mark?
> What could've been implemented to avoid divorce?
> Was pride a part of their downfall?

There was a man named Jeremiah who was married to a very strong-willed woman named Kendra. Kendra didn't listen to a word Jeremiah said and always had a refutation for any statement he made, but their relationship didn't start out like this.

They were high school sweethearts and had it *made*. Jeremiah was the football champion, and Kendra was the star cheerleader. She lived by the saying, "My momma didn't raise no fool," and played hard to get. When they met initially, Kendra thought that Jeremiah only wanted *one thing* and made it clear that she was not that kind of *girl*. After Jeremiah's persistent pursuit, and leaving gifts in her locker, she finally agreed to go on one date with him. Not too long after their first date, they made arrangements for another and even more after that. The connection they made on each date confirmed their 'forever', and they agreed to follow each other to the same college. Luckily, their athletic ability landed them scholarships and they both stayed on the Dean's List. All of their peers deemed them as *relationship goals*.

On the night of their final college homecoming game, Jeremiah proposed to Kendra and shortly afterwards, he received offers to play professional football. Even though Kendra was excited for him, she didn't want to give up her dreams of becoming a nurse. Being the type of person Jeremiah was, he didn't want to come between that, so he committed to helping Kendra start her own Assisted Living Community (ALC) in the city where he was recruited to play pro-football. The center became very successful and so did Jeremiah's football career.

Unfortunately, two years later, Jeremiah sustained a knee injury that put him out for a few seasons, resulting in him losing the opportunity to renew his contract. So, he decided to put his accounting degree to work and opened up his own accounting firm, providing auditing services to private companies. During this time, Kendra was expecting their first child. She knew Jeremiah was intelligent and believed that his company would be successful, and it was. Fast forward to year four of their marriage, they were three kids in and working at the ALC full time became too much for Kendra. Jeremiah recognized her stress and they both agreed to sell the ALC to Kendra's sister who was also a nurse, so the business could stay in the family. The ALC was doing well, but they took a hit when one of their biggest insurance agencies went bankrupt. This crushed Kendra, but Jeremiah refused to let her stress over it and assured her his business would be able to meet any gaps in their monthly expenses. It did for months.

One day, while Jeremiah was in his accounting office, he was approached by an old college friend who was trying to start up her auditing business. He spoke with her, provided her tips and out of trust, gave her a redacted copy of his initial business plan to assist her with hers. Not too long after their interaction, Jeremiah received several overwhelming emails from agencies he was contracted with, requesting to end their contract due to a better offer they received. Jeremiah wasn't found of begging, but as a businessman, he asked what the competitor contractor was offering and soon found out that the *old friend* he helped, composed a better offer to all of his contracts, which many of his clients accepted.

This crushed Jeremiah's business and created a large lapse in customers. It was causing him more money to keep the business afloat, so he ultimately decided to close down. As a result, it wasn't too long before Jeremiah and Kendra's savings were depleted as the needs of their children seemed to sky rocket. They had to downsize in a major way and tried to adjust to their new normal as quickly as possible for the sake of their children.

Over time, Kendra grew tired of not living as *comfortable* as she used to and resented having to pick back up several shifts at the ALC just to pay the bills. It was hard for Jeremiah to find work with his football and entrepreneurship background, so he worked odd jobs to help contribute to their expenses. Kendra would constantly scoff at the money Jeremiah brought in by making snide remarks such as, "We have real bills so we need real money. Not this pocket change you're bringing in." Anytime Jeremiah tried to defend himself and make it known that he was trying, Kendra would cut him off and tell him how unreliable he was and that his pursuit of her in High School wasn't worth the sacrifices she now had to make. Despite this, Jeremiah still put in as much effort as he could to meet their financial needs and keep their marriage strong.

However, months of her belittling turned into years and Jeremiah grew tired of trying to *please* her. As a result, he began to focus solely on their children: taking them to school, helping them with their homework, putting them to bed at night and then going straight to the basement, which became his home. Neither he nor Kendra addressed this internal move-out and they only spoke when it pertained to the children. To prevent any further stress and pressure, they also agreed not to speak about their marriage issues to their family, and for Jeremiah to look into corporate accounting firms for positions.

Jeremiah applied for accounting jobs consistently as agreed, but began to lose hope because nothing seemed to come through. But just when Jeremiah was about to call it quits, he received a call from one of the companies he had contracted with, in his own business, offering him an accounting position at his firm. Jeremiah accepted with no hesitation. The salary was great, but he knew the money would go straight to all the debt they had accumulated after losing their primary incomes.

With excitement that he hadn't had in a while, he told Kendra the good news. Instead of congratulations, she said, "Great!" With much sarcasm and let him know that she was going to stop contributing to the bills as a way to *repay* herself for the years of his lack and her sacrifices. This created an even greater wedge between them and they both grew even colder towards one another. They were both very stubborn. Jeremiah refused to go back to that boy he was in High School who had a never-ending pursuit for the girl of his dreams, and Kendra did not show the slightest interest in reconciliation.

Consequently, after six months of this coldness, Kendra filed for a legal separation and moved out with the children. While their marriage was taking a negative turn, Jeremiah's career was taking a positive one. He was promoted to Vice President of the company which tripled his salary. He again, shared the good news with Kendra but she still displayed a careless attitude towards him and bid him a 'good for you' congratulations. When it was time for the children to visit Jeremiah, Kendra would drop the kids off and keep it moving, never looking Jeremiah's way.

Deep down, Kendra wanted her family to be reunited but she didn't know where or how to start. She was so used to him being the one to pursue her, so, she never learned how to show him that he was also desirable. Kendra's harsh words during their trials not only killed his confidence, but also the *worth* he saw in chasing her. Even when he would attempt to do something nice, she would respond with criticism of what he could have or should have done *better*, or not respond at all. So, when his chasing completely stopped, her waiting did also.

Kendra filed for a divorce after they had been separated for a year, and requested half of everything. Being the man that he was, well what was left of him, Jeremiah gave her more than half of everything and just desired full custody of their children. Kendra was resistant at first but agreed once they came to a common ground on her being able to see the children. From there, they rarely spoke directly to each other. Mainly through a mutual party when it pertained to their children.

Two years after their divorce was finalized, Jeremiah was open to dating again. He grew in attraction to one of the auditors at his firm; however, he never liked mixing business with pleasure. To Jeremiah's surprise, this co-worker was also interested in him, but had the same reservations. However, she was leaving that company for a better offer at one of their sister firms. This was a good enough *business* distance for them and they went out on a few dates. He learned that she had two kids of her own, and had broken off an engagement six months ago. She told him the relationship was well over before the engagement and that she finally accepted the fact that after 10 years, her fiancé was never going to make her his wife. Even though she didn't blame it all on her ex-fiancé, sharing her role in making him *comfortable,* she talked about her frustrations about being led on for so long for his convenience.

Jeremiah shared his story and highlighted the similarities in their experiences.. Months went by and she remained just as consistent in their relationship as did he. Her effort in making their relationship work was equal to his which was a new experience for Jeremiah. He was used to being the only one pedaling on a two-seat bicycle and because of this, he knew he desired to solidify their relationship.

Out of respect, Jeremiah told Kendra directly of his intentions of marrying this new woman, and Kendra also shared that she was seeing someone. Kendra didn't seem bothered by this news and told Jeremiah she was happy for him. But when she walked away from that conversation, she was flooded with memories of what used to be between them. Her eyes filled with tears almost every time she dropped their children off and, even though she had been dating, she often confided that it never felt the same, in that Jeremiah was the only person she had met with a relentless pursuit of her.

She saw how happy Jeremiah was and respected how uplifting his new soon to be wife was. As Kendra was going through her healing process, she apologized for not being the support Jeremiah needed most when times got hard and for any hurt she'd caused him. He apologized for the role he played by giving up and not pushing harder. Kendra expressed how their financial hurdle scared her because Jeremiah was always able to provide, and how that change so drastically *changed* her as well. She recognized that it was *too late* to reconcile their marriage and expressed how she had to heal from the feelings of guilt and regret of her not being more willing to *fix it* before reconciliation was off the table completely.

This story could have gone so many ways, but I hope you understand the point I want to drive home. Don't wait until it's too late. You can make the decision to fix your marriage right now, before signing the divorce papers and before calculating what he *owes* you. While you sit and think of all the reasons to leave, also take the time to think of all the reasons you may have given him to want to leave. Is he more confident because of you? Or is he more hesitant, doubtful and secretive because of you? If a stranger on the street asked him what was the last kind word his wife spoke to him, would he have to hurt his brain to think of an answer? How have your words and attitude contributed to the *issues* in your marriage?

If it happens to be *too late* for you, and your divorce is finalized or both of you have moved on and you're sure both of you are past the point of reconciliation, I want you to be intentional about not repeating the cycle. Don't continue to do and say the things the way you did in your previous marriage. Really examine yourself and take heed to the constant flaws that friends or family point out to you either jokingly or seriously. Do people say you've *always* been impatient, quick-tempered, sassy or strong-willed? If you're reading this book, chances are that you are old enough to know when an *attitude* is no longer cute and that you have an important role to play in becoming a better you. How will you change those previous negative behaviors so that they won't damage your next relationship? How will you be intentional about *not* bringing in your baggage and assumptions from your previous relationship(s)? These are questions you have to honestly answer for yourself, and develop real goals and plans.

No one is perfect: we all have flaws. However, when we are blinded or in denial that our flaws are damaging to ourselves and others, we run the risk of bleeding on everyone who tries to love us, even our children. A band-aid won't cut it, sis; you need emotional surgery and I know of only One who can effectively do the job: Jesus.

> *He shall call upon Me, and I will answer him; I will be with him in trouble; I will deliver him and honor him. With long life I will satisfy him, And show him My salvation* (Psalm 91:15-16 NKJV).

Then they cried out to the Lord in their trouble, And He saved them out of their distresses. He sent His word and healed them, And delivered them from their destruction (Psalm 107:19-20 NKJV).

13

Lovers in a Pandemic: Tried and True

My husband and I got married a month before the Covid-19 pandemic took its toll on the Nation. As you know, this was not the most *ideal* situation for anyone. With us being newlyweds, we wanted to be in Cancun honeymooning and spending our Friday's on date nights, but that wasn't the case. Instead, a lot of our days were spent making sure that our household and families were *good*. Despite this, I believe that we grew closer than any honeymoon or date night could have ever brought us.

I always desired for us to have the ability to work from home, but never in the capacity and constraints the pandemic made us. My ideal tele-working situation would've still allowed me to go out, run errands, and even take a nice vacay while still getting work done. Waking up next to each other, going to sleep next to each other, working next to each other, not being able to really go out and get *space*, was a new and different experience that I can definitely say I'm grateful for. Some people may be saying, of course you loved it, you were newlyweds.

However, I beg to differ. Being in such close and consistent proximity could've been detrimental. We could have come to some assumption that we married wrong, or that we hated each other because there were some moments where he absolutely got on my nerves, and there were moments where I absolutely got on his. However, we didn't break in those moments and the reason goes far beyond the fact that we were *newlyweds*. It's a testament to our foundation, which is Jesus Christ. We took a vow before God and committed to one another for life. We knew hard times would come and we knew that it would not always be sunshine, rainbows and morning sex. We KNEW marriage was work before we made that commitment, and in times of frustration, we remembered that commitment.

What commitment do you need to re-visit in your marriage? Is it going back to the basics and being as intentional as you were in your honeymoon stage? Is it dying to yourself and being selfless? Is it remembering the vows you made at the altar and making the decision to honor them? If you're dating or engaged, is the commitment you need to re-visit waiting until you walk down that aisle to share your bodies with one another? If you're single, is the commitment you need to re-visit not to allow that same guy to continue to lead you on, only to lead you astray or cause you to lower your standards?

No matter what our relationship statuses are, there is a commitment in it. Are we sticking to it or running away? Are we changing the guidelines of our commitment when it's convenient for us? A commitment is a commitment. It doesn't change just because your feelings changed. Feelings come and go; that's why it's important not to live in your feelings or make commitments/decisions based on *emotions*. Once that fire, passion and adrenalin are gone, so is the commitment. When you come down from that emotion, you may find yourself trying to fill the holes and spaces your emotions left, or kicking yourself because of the decision you made and you can't take it back.

We must make commitments with a sound mind. A sound mind allows us to separate wisdom from feelings. When we make sound commitments, wisdom tells us that even when I don't feel like it or even if the other person is not holding up their end, I still must do the right thing. Feelings tell us, I'm in it until their actions change my mind. That's not how it is with God; no matter how our actions make Him feel, He's still right there loving us relentlessly. And if our marriages are supposed to be a reflection of Christ's relationship with us, we should strive to implement that same commitment and grace with our spouses.

When a pandemic or tragic event hits your commitment/marriage, how will you respond? Are you sticking to it or straying from it? Some singles probably feared that this pandemic would rob them of the opportunity of marriage or even experiencing God's best in love. As a result, some settled for a quarantine-buddy which was the *true* delay, not the quarantine. Some marriages were put to the test as couples came to terms with who they really married or who their spouse had become, which led to separations, divorces or talks of it. Unfortunately, we don't know what kind of hardships life may bring, but we know they will come. And because we know they will come, we should spend our fruitful seasons preparing for those hard times.

Every marriage and relationship require a *storm kit*. A storm kit is a kit in which you store all the necessities that will help you get through a natural disaster. It contains your basic needs such as water, non-perishable food items, flashlights, batteries and a few other things. You keep your storm kit in a safe, but accessible place; so when the storm comes, you know how to access it quickly to ensure your survival. Our marital storm kits serve the same purpose, helping us ensure our marriage's survival through the storm. These are some items our marital storm kits should have:

- Prayer: When storms come, their expiration date is not always made known to

  man. So, it's important to know how to fight and breakthrough in prayer

  unbound by time. Simply placing tape on the windows won't keep them from breaking. One, you have to know how to board your windows by casting out the enemy, and two, how to bring light into a dark place by setting the atmosphere.

- Ready knowledge of God's Word: When you are in a storm, it is not the time to *learn* survival skills. You must go in equipped with the tactics on how to fight and protect — which is, talking back to the enemy with the Word of God. He won't sit and wait while you Google a Scripture to defeat him. Plant God's Word in your heart, BEFOREHAND. You must also be able to survive off of the food you stored prior to the storm—which is being able to recall and speak back to the storm what God told you before the rain came.

- Discernment: In a storm, it is never safe to play the guessing game. Guessing will get you wiped out. Having discernment will let you know when to take high ground before a flood or when to retreat — this means holding your tongue and knowing when to address something. This also means to stop digging in dead ground, *trying* to find things in his phone when you've come up empty-handed a million times already. That's fleshy and impulsive. If there is truly something to find, discernment will lead you to it at just the right time.

- Forgiveness: It's so hard to get through a storm, but even more so when you're locked in a safe house with someone you have so much resentment towards. My best friend and maid-of-honor shared the following advice from her late grandfather that was so pivotal at our wedding: "You must enter your relationship prepared to forgive because there will come a point where each of you has to be forgiven." You will need your spouse's forgiveness one day and vice versa. Don't feel so entitled to his forgiveness when you aren't even willing to extend the same grace. Without forgiveness, you can be sure that, if the storm doesn't take you out, bitterness and unforgiveness will.

- Communication: In a storm, it's so easy to lose control and panic. However, when you know how to communicate calmly and effectively, you're able to settle emotions and safely instruct others on how to reach safe ground. In marriage, this would be getting back to a loving and respectful place by knowing *how* to say what needs to be said. Choosing to communicate harshly will only lead to cycles of storms and eventually, a wipeout.

How can I prepare for the storm if I don't know it's coming? For my singles ladies, prepare the same way you are preparing for your husband, but aren't sure when he's coming. You are intentional about learning how to cook, intentional about your appearance etc. So, transfer that same effort to getting planted in the knowledge and Word of the Lord. If you're already married and are currently encountering storms, take that same energy you give to arguments, down talking him to your girlfriends, and eyeing the *new guy,* to your prayer closet, and let the Lord work wonders for you.

In order to get through a storm, not only do you need a storm kit but you need a survivor's mindset. You have to make up in your mind that your marriage or in your singleness, you will win, you will heal from the heartbreak, that God will send you your spouse, and that the hand of God is greater than the hand that is against your marriage or singleness. A made-up mind means being committed to the win, and not allowing anything contrary to that in your space. I'm not saying that it will be an easy fight because it won't, but it will be worth the fight once you see the glory that God will get from it as well as the new love that comes out of it.

I know that you may be tired of fighting, tired of praying; but don't let the storm(s) overtake you. Rather, you overtake the storm. Your husband/ future husband deserves the best and healed version of you and more importantly, you deserve the best and healed version of you. Fight more to hold back the fire of that tongue and fight less to prove a point. Nothing grows under scrutiny: it only shrinks. But encouraging words build up and blossom. This means no more talking down about your spouse or marriage to yourself and others. This means no more looking at your spouse with eyes of disdain and disgust. This means loving your spouse and letting him love you back.

If that is a struggle for you, ask God to change the way you see your spouse and your marriage. Ask Him to help you have eyes for your husband only, and to strengthen your desire for him. We can over-complicate the things that we feel we're allowed to ask or tell God; but I assure you that He is concerned about everything that concerns you. He desires for your marriage to work. So, don't hide how you *really* feel or what you really struggle with in your marriage. Bring it to Him so He can reveal, heal and restore.

14

The One

The last thing I want anyone to get from this book is that I have conquered all of the areas I have discussed. I haven't. There is still work I have to do, and it is a constant dying-to-self kind of journey. When I was writing this book, there were times I didn't even want to work on certain chapters because I was still developing in those areas. There were times that God would really put fire under me to write, and I wouldn't because my husband and I had gotten into an argument and I didn't say or do the most loving of things.

But I learned that God allowed this book to amplify and highlight the areas of my life that still need some adjustment; and those areas went beyond my husband upsetting me. It went back to the root of why certain things angered or triggered me right back to the cycles of rebellion that were present in my childhood.

Through writing this book, being a Licensed Social Worker, Therapist and knowing the importance of total wellness, I painfully learned the truth about *me*. I learned that I was still broken in certain areas and the *specific* ways I bled on others. I even learned the painful reality: that 'if I had been healed' when I entered certain relationships, I wouldn't have left an ugly stain on them. I learned that I had very deep feelings of anger towards people in my family and despised the way I grew up, which were projected in other ways. I learned that I desired to be on people's *approved* list just to truly feel that I was *called,* and I hated it. I learned that the reason behind my drive and ambition was more than just a desire to be *successful.* It was fueled by the lack I had in my childhood, and the things I felt I should never have had to *want* for. I learned the depth of my toxicity and it was a painful reality to face.

This reality resulted in tears and frustration, but through it all, I'm glad I learned and the important thing is that I LEARNED. I'm not perfect, but I'm nowhere near who I use to be and I'm the closest I have ever been to becoming the *me* God called me to be. Being aware and acting on that awareness was the very key to my total wellness. It may be the key to yours too.

You know how we've left a carbon footprint on the earth with our toxic habits of not recycling, wasting energy and pollution? Well, those are some of the same characteristics we carry in our personal lives, which causes us to leave a carbon footprint on people closest to us, or those who try to get close to us. Are you aware of your carbon footprint on people? Yes, I know you have pain, too, and I want you to know that I acknowledge that. You deserve to be healed and free. And a part of that healing and freedom is coming to terms with the damage that *your damage* has caused.

How are you going to make sure you set yourself and your family up for a better emotional wellbeing? How will you make sure you break the negative cycles from your childhood and even in your present? When will your children see you and your spouse have a healthy disagreement that actually has a meaningful, healthy resolution? Are you aware that those same nasty habits you produce in your marriage are impacting your children, both born and unborn? Ending the unhealthy cycles has to start somewhere. So, why not let it be with you? You don't have to be a product of your environment, and I want you to make the decision to not blame anyone else for where you are. That mindset will keep you stuck.

Whether you grew up in a seemingly healthy household or an unhealthy one, I'm sure you saw areas where changes could be implemented for the better. So, initiate those changes. Be the one to do that *different thing* everyone else in your family has been scared of doing, especially if it's led by God. Don't shrink back because of the disapprovals you fear are waiting for you if you step out, and make that move. Just do it. Be the one to have that successful marriage. Be the one who gets married God's way. Be the one who chooses to make your husband a plate at the family cookout despite the *seasoned* women side-eyeing you. Be the one to take your family to counseling even though people say *we* don't do that.

Whatever that cycle breaking change is in your family or for you, be *the one* to implement it. There is an entire generation waiting to see if *it* can be done and how. Show them just how possible it is, and above all, show yourself how possible it is, even though you may have some doubt about the possibilities, too. Once you're able to walk through the door to a better you, don't close it to those behind you, unless there are people trying to bring you back down. Otherwise, show them what you weren't shown and tell them what you weren't told.

A part of being a healthier and whole you is not holding back the *how to* knowledge from others. I'm not saying you should let people drain you. What I'm saying is that you should help those who truly want to be or do better, and I pray that God strengthens your discernment in order to know the difference. Also, don't be surprised or discouraged when people confuse your *healthy* optimism with a lack of humility. Misery and toxicity love company and it's okay when you choose to no longer join them. Never let them make you feel guilty about being a better you and also, please be sure to not get on a high horse, looking down at those you *surpassed*.

If 2020 has taught me anything, it's the importance of humility. I'm confident that the lessons of 2020 will be relevant for a lifetime. So, whatever year you find yourself reading or rereading this book, just reflect back on all God showed and exposed to you during that time, specifically during the pandemic when all we had was time.

Have you put the blinders back on, or are you walking in the clear vision that God gave you? If 2020 didn't bring you the clear vision you needed, marriage definitely will. If you're single or engaged, you don't have to wait until then. Marriage has its own challenges in itself, so why bring anything extra into the mix? Work to become a better, whole you *now*. If you're married, it's time to stop fighting change. It's time to get up and make up your mind. You're either in or you're out. If you're in, you cannot keep circling back to issues that should have *been* forgiven and let go of by now. If you made the choice to forgive, put some action to that and move forward in the steps that are needed to make your marriage healthier. If you're out, please do not take that baggage and unpack it at someone else's door (see *Divorce* section). Go unpack it at the Lord's feet and stay there until He says otherwise. Don't rush into another relationship or some other void filler. Take the *real time* you need to heal.

Today, **we will** take responsibility, today we will implement change, and today, we will put an end to all the cycles we've found ourselves in, whether intentional or unintentional. Today, we fight for our marriages and believe the best about our (future) spouses and ourselves.

*"Every day that you choose your marriage, you take off and surpass the limits you were bound by yesterday. Every day that you choose your marriage, is another day you have chosen to be **the one**."* - Eliyah Britto